Incredible Elfego Baca

Good Man, Bad Man of the Old West

Howard Bryan

Foreword by Rudolfo Anaya

Clear Light Publishers
Santa Fe, New Mexico

Clear Light Publishers
823 Don Diego
Santa Fe, New Mexico 87501

Library of Congress Cataloging in Publication Data

Bryan, Howard.
    Incredible Elfego Baca: good man, bad man of the old west /
Howard Bryan ; foreword by Rudolfo Anaya.
        p. cm.
        ISBN 0–940666–34–0 : $22.95
        1. Baca, Elfego, 1864–1945. 2. Sheriffs—New Mexico—Biogra-
phy.   3. Crime—New Mexico—History. 4. New Mexico—History—1848–   I. Title.
F801.B15B79   1993
978.9'052'092—dc20   93–5332
[B]   CIP

First Edition
10 9 8 7 6 5 4 3 2 1

Designed by Irving Warhaftig
Printed in U.S.A.
Baker Johnson,
Dexter, Michigan

Printed on recycled paper which meets the minimum requirements of American National Standard for Information Sciences—Permanence of Paper for printed library materials, ANSIZ39, 48–1984

In a country where, in the past,
picturesque characters have been the rule
rather than the exception, it is doubtful
if a more picturesque character than
Elfego Baca has ever lived.

Albuquerque Morning Journal, February 1, 1915

Contents

Foreword

As a young university student in 1959 I remember taking a break from my studies to join my family around the television set once a week. The show we watched was "The Nine Lives of Elfego Baca," a Walt Disneyesque series which atempted to capture the life of this famous lawman from Socorro County.

The show had the usual appeal of a cowboy/western/adventure series, but we also watched for other reasons. Here, for the first time of television history, was a New Mexican, one of our own, standing up to the bad guys! Never before had Hollywood portrayed a Nuevo Mexicano as a hero, and very few have appeared since.

Since then I have been haunted by the ghost of Elfego Baca. I have wanted to know more about the life and times of this complex man, so I thank Howard Bryan for putting together this very readable book on Elfego. Howard has a nose for news, having spent most of his life on the Albuquerque beat. He knows intimately the old friends and haunts of Elfego. The portrait he draws is true. Warts and all.

Elfego wasn't the hero Walt Disney made him to be. Oh, we can wish he was, but life after the Civil War in the New Mexican territory was violent, and it spawned complex men. Perhaps Elfego mirrored his times as much as Billy the Kid. But give me the real man Howard presents rather than the Disney caricature anytime. With faults and good points, I'll take the man for what he was. Howard presents the facts with care and sensitivity.

When the time calls for heroes, the myth of the hero

1

becomes bigger than the man, and in our time we do need heroes. For me Elfego Baca has always been a hero — both the man and the myth. As a young man he stood up to injustice. So, I take his good points and excuse some of his follies.

As a character says in one of my novels, "They ought to build a statue of Elfego Baca." We should. We seem to honor too few of our heroes. My novel is fiction, of course, but it shows how history affects our stories today. History makes us yearn for those men or women who once set things right.

I hope Howard's book is the raw granite, the inspiration from which we can begin to carve an understanding of the man. At any rate, this book begins to fill the void in our history.

Gracias, Howard.

Rudolfo Anaya

Introduction

While practicing law in Albuquerque, New Mexico, according to an oft-told story, Elfego Baca received a telegram from a client in El Paso, Texas, reading, "Need you at once. Have just been charged with murder;" to which Baca responded with a telegram reading, "Leaving at once with three eyewitnesses."

This story, with a number of variations, was one of Baca's favorite tales, and one that helped to create his lasting image as one of New Mexico's most colorful and legendary figures. On the eve of his seventy-fifth birthday in 1940, however, Baca admitted to a reporter for the *Albuquerque Tribune* that this telegram exchange never occurred but he was "stuck with the story and could not do anything about it."

"I absolutely had nothing to do with this tale, but it's a good one," he told the newspaper in a rare instance of denying a good story about himself.

The 1937 edition of *Who's Who in New Mexico* identified Baca as both a "good man" and a "bad man," a description that he probably relished and that reflected the general opinion of him at the time. To some, he was admired as a tough hombre who championed the cause of the poor and the Hispanic citizens of New Mexico; to others, he was ridiculed as an unethical and gun-toting lawyer who lived on the reputation he had achieved as a frontier gunfighter who was said to have single-handedly fought off eighty bloodthirsty cowboys who fired four thousand shots at him without effect.

A legend in his own time, a folk hero after his death,

Baca was a true product of the Western frontier, a man whose action-filled life would have earned him a place in history and folklore even without the exaggerations with which he and others saw fit to embellish his remarkable career. Referred to as a "ruffian" during his youth, Baca embarked on a long and varied career as a lawyer, private detective, sheriff and deputy sheriff, county clerk, school superintendent, mayor, district attorney, and candidate for New Mexico governor and the United States House of Representatives. In each instance, his service was not without controversy. Three times he was tried for murder but acquitted each time, and he and others were tried and acquitted on charges of conspiracy against the United States.

Much of what is known about Baca's eventful life stems from a political pamphlet that he first issued in Albuquerque in 1924 in announcing his candidacy for the Democratic nomination for judge of the Second Judicial District and that he reprinted with a few revisions as an office seeker in 1940 and 1944. In this pamphlet, which proved so popular with voters that he stopped giving copies away and started selling them for ten cents each, Baca provided highlights of his life in his own inimitable style. Despite the popularity of the pamphlet, however, he was unsuccessful in these election bids.

Kyle S. Crichton, an Albuquerque advertising executive, used the pamphlet and subsequent interviews with Baca to write an expanded version of Baca's life in a 219-page book, *Law and Order Ltd., The Rousing Life of Elfego Baca*, published in 1928 by the New Mexican Publishing Corporation in Santa Fe. This entertaining book was the product of two fertile imaginations, those of the author and his subject, and it includes numerous episodes that

4

historians would be hard-pressed to verify. Coincidental with the completion of the manuscript for the present book, the Texas Western Press at El Paso released a new book, *Elfego Baca in Life and Legend,* a scholarly study of Baca's life by Larry D. Ball, professor of history at Arkansas State University.

Baca's remarkable life spanned eighty years, from the closing battles of the Civil War to the end of World War II and the dawn of the nuclear age. No period of his four score years was without drama, controversy, or humor, from his kidnapping by an Indian war party in the first year of his life to his campaign for district attorney in the last year of his life.

I did not have the pleasure of meeting Baca, for he died in Albuquerque three years before I arrived there to begin my employment as a reporter and columnist for the *Albuquerque Tribune.* At the time, Baca anecdotes were a favorite topic of conversation among all New Mexicans who had known him, admirers and critics alike, and they remain so today.

In this book I have relied to a large extent on the Baca pamphlets and the Crichton biography, supplementing them, wherever possible, with newspaper articles, court and other official documents, published eyewitness accounts of Baca's activities, and interviews and conversations with pioneers who knew him.

In many cases, it is impossible to separate fact from fiction, as Baca often provided varying and exaggerated accounts of episodes in his career while remaining vague or silent about others. Like many pioneers of his era, he knew how to make a good story even better.

A photograph of the San Miguel Church in Socorro, New Mexico, where Elfego Baca was baptized in 1865. (Courtesy of Museum of New Mexico, negative no. 11434).

Here Comes Elfego!

Elfego Baca was a gifted and witty storyteller, as evidenced in his political pamphlets. In telling of his birth, he wrote:

> *Elfego Baca was born on the 27th day of February, 1865, at Socorro, New Mexico. He was born under peculiar circumstances. His mother, Juanita Baca, married when 19 years old. She was with other growing girls playing [a] game called at that time "Las Iglesias," a game which is now called "soft ball" game. Juanita mother of Elfego was short and stubby and [when] one of the balls [was] hit by one of the girls in the direction of Juanita, Elfego's mother, Juanita jumped up to stop the ball and here comes Elfego. From the spot Juanita and Elfego both were taken into the house, and both were taken under medical care.*

Although records of the Catholic Church in Socorro indicate that Baca was baptized on February 15, 1865, when he was five days old, he apparently thought he was born on February 27, as he observed that day as his birthday during his entire life.

Socorro, at the time of Baca's birth in 1865, was a squalid village of several hundred Spanish-speaking citizens, although it was soon to experience a boom brought on by a surge in mining activities in the mountains west of town and the coming of the Atchison, Topeka and Santa

Fe Railroad in 1880. Situated on the west bank of the Rio Grande in south-central New Mexico, the community was established by Hispanic settlers in 1816 over the ruins of the Piro Indian Pueblo of Pilabo and its seventeenth century mission church, Nuestra Senora de Pilabo del Socorro, which had been abandoned during the Pueblo Indian Revolt against Spanish rule in 1680. In 1851 the village was designated the seat of immense Socorro County, a vast expanse of mountains and plains inhabited principally by roving bands of Apache Indians.

Baca said that he was one year old when his father, Francisco Baca, a Socorro County cattle rancher, moved the family to Topeka, Kansas, traveling by ox train. While camped in the Estancia Valley, northeast of Socorro, he said, he was kidnapped by a party of Navajo Indians who assaulted the camp but was returned to his parents unharmed several days later. At the time, 1866, the Navajos were being held in captivity on the Bosque Redondo Reservation at Fort Sumner, on the Pecos River east of the Estancia Valley, but groups of them periodically escaped from the reservation to conduct raids in the region.

Baca was vague about his early years in Kansas, the reason for the move, and the length of his stay. He indicated that his father embarked on the nearly one-thousand-mile trek to Topeka to give his family the benefits of an education that Socorro could not offer. When asked years later about how much education he had had, his answer was, "Not much." His father apparently worked as a minor contractor in Topeka, where Elfego was reared in a frontier, English-speaking environment.

Baca wrote that his mother died in Topeka on March 1, 1872, shortly after the death of his sister, Eloisa, on

February 18, and shortly before the death of his brother, Herminio, on March 9. He noted that all three died within one month but gave no cause of their demise.

When his mother died, Baca wrote, his father sent him and his older brother, Abdenago, back to Socorro to live with relatives while he remained in Topeka to close his affairs. Elfego would have been seven years old in 1872, but he later indicated that he was fifteen years old when he returned to Socorro, which would have been in 1880. Since Baca said he could speak very little Spanish at age sixteen, he probably returned to Socorro at age fifteen, for it is doubtful that he could have been living in a Spanish-speaking community since age seven without being fluent in the native language of his relatives and friends.

A nephew, Abe B. Baca of Socorro, was quoted in a 1981 interview as saying that Elfego was placed in a Topeka orphanage after his mother died and that Abdenago, who was five years older than Elfego, went to work in Colorado before returning to Socorro, where he later served as county assessor for fifteen years. Abe, who was a son of Abdenago, said that while Elfego was attending school in Topeka he became acquainted with Charles Curtis, five years his senior, who later was to serve thirty-four years as a United States senator and congressman from Kansas and vice president of the United States during the administration of President Herbert Hoover. Boyhood pals, they were to renew their acquaintanceship years later during Baca's periodic business trips to the nation's capital.

It is probable, then, that Baca returned to Socorro from Topeka in 1880, the same year that the Atchison, Topeka and Santa Fe Railroad reached his hometown from Kansas, eight years after the death of his mother.

Elfego Baca at about the age of 16. (Courtesy Museum of New Mexico, negative no. 48462.)

Some Early Escapades

Socorro, in 1880, was embarking on its boom period, its population swelling with the influx of large numbers of English-speaking settlers who referred to themselves as "Americans" and to the native Hispanics as "Mexicans." Baca, as a native Hispanic who was fluent only in English, felt more comfortable among the English-speaking newcomers, and, as he was to prove later, he certainly was not intimidated by their superior attitude.

Like many raconteurs who were in New Mexico in 1881 and shortly before, Baca claimed an acquaintanceship with Billy the Kid. According to his account:

> *My grand parents had cattle and I went to be a cowboy. At that time I must have been about 16 years old when I met Billy the Kid in a round-up at a certain place northeast of Socorro called "La Parida Ranch." There were over forty cowboys gathered, branding cattle, etc. Billy must have been at that time about 17 years old and he talked good Spanish and I couldn't talk but very little Spanish. As a matter of fact I was afraid of what they called Mexicans.*

Baca wrote that one day he and Billy rode north from the ranch to Isleta Pueblo, about fourteen miles south of Albuquerque, stabled their horses there, and rode into Albuquerque on a Santa Fe Railroad section cart. Upon their arrival in Albuquerque, he said, they camped under a cottonwood tree by a saloon at the southwest corner of Railroad (now Central) Avenue and First Street. He continued:

> *Billy and I were wandering [sic] what we were going to do when here comes a policeman and shot a man about five or six times. The policeman went into a saloon and called the boys to have a drink. About that time here comes [Sheriff] Perfecto Armijo and said, "Who killed that man out there?" The policeman said, "I did, what about it?" Perfecto then caught him by the left hand by the back of the shirt collar and with the right hand from the rear end of his body and picked him up just like a cat will pick up a mouse. This policeman was tried and convicted to be hung and was hung.*

The episode Baca described here could only have been the unprovoked killing of Charles D. Campbell, a railroad carpenter, by Milton J. Yarberry, Albuquerque's town marshal, which occurred on the evening of June 18, 1881, less than a month before Billy the Kid was shot to death by Sheriff Pat Garrett at Fort Sumner, New Mexico. The shooting of Campbell occurred only yards from where Baca said he and Billy were camped. Yarberry was convicted of murder and was hanged.

Baca said that he and Billy, in search of some excitement, went to the Martinez Saloon in Albuquerque's Old Town, "where there was dancing, gambling and every other thing." He said Billy thought the place was too quiet and began firing his little but noisy Bulldog repeater pistol into the air, much to the annoyance of Deputy Sheriff Cornelio Murphy. Baca said Murphy searched both of them twice without finding a weapon, the reason being that Billy, after firing each shot into the air, quickly hid his pistol under the stiff derby hat he was wearing.

"Then Billy and I continued to stay around Albuquerque and vicinity perhaps a couple of weeks," Baca continued. "I went to work for a man named Francisco Apodaca over here in Barelas [at the south edge of Albuquerque]. His son Pedro and I hauled all the ham for the roundhouse of the A.T. & S. F."

Most of Billy the Kid's many biographers have been skeptical of Baca's story, noting that all evidence indicates that the Kid, who was at least six years older than Baca, was hiding out in and around Fort Sumner, about one hundred and sixty miles southeast of Albuquerque, during the period Baca had him calling attention to himself in Albuquerque. The Kid was killed at Fort Sumner on July 14, 1881, at the age of twenty-one. Crichton's biography of Baca said that "Billy had not yet begun his famous career" when the sixteen-year-old Baca met him, yet in 1881 the Kid was a notorious outlaw with a $500 price on his head and was near the end of his famous career.

Since there were several young desperadoes at the time who were known as Billy the Kid (or merely Kid), it is possible that Baca's friend was not the notorious William H. Bonney of Lincoln County War fame.

Baca was engaged in a number of other adventures and escapades shortly after his return to New Mexico, including the rescue of his father from a county jail in 1881 and the unauthorized closing down of a cousin's store sometime in the 1880s.

Elfego's father, Francisco Baca, following his return from Topeka, became town marshal of the Valencia County community of Belen, about forty-five miles north of Socorro, and in that capacity incurred the enmity of a powerful political family (probably the Luna family) by punching one of its members in the nose. After shooting to death two boisterous cowboys in Belen in December 1880, two murder indictments were returned against him. He was placed in the county jail at Los Lunas, ten miles north of Belen, pending trial on the two indictments.

In May 1881, a district court jury in Los Lunas, seat of Valencia County, found Francisco guilty of murder in the fifth degree in connection with one of the indictments, and he was remanded to jail to await trial on the second indictment.

Elfego, believing that his father was the victim of a political vendetta, told Crichton that he decided to rescue him from the jail and that he proceeded to Los Lunas with a young companion, whom he identified only as Chavez.

The jail, on the ground floor of a two-story court-house building and located beneath the courtroom, was left unguarded when Baca and his friend arrived at night, as the jailer had left to attend a religious function. Finding a ladder, the two climbed through a second floor window and proceeded to a spot in the jury room directly above the cell in which Francisco and several other prisoners were being held. Sawing a hole in the floor, Baca and Chavez lifted the prisoners up through the opening, and all left the building and concealed themselves in some high grass in a field directly across the road from the courthouse entrance.

All the next day, while eating some food taken from the courthouse and watermelons found in the field, they watched as armed posses left the courthouse in search of the escaped prisoners. When darkness came they split up, the two Bacas and Chavez heading south for Socorro and the other escapees heading north for Albuquerque. Francisco Baca went on south to Ysleta, Texas, near El Paso, where he spent the next seven years with a brother who operated a store there, Elfego said.

A contemporary newspaper account of the jailbreak indicates that it occurred on or about the night of June 24, 1881, and that outside help was not suspected at the time. On June 26, 1881, the *Daily New Mexican*, published in Santa Fe, ran this account under the headline "More Jail Birds Flown":

> *A day or two ago the jail of Valencia County was broken and delivered of all the occupants save one poor unfortunate who through the treacherous conduct of his companions got left. The jail contained Francisco Baca, John Pearee [Pearce?], the man with the euphonious alias, Thacker, the wife murderer, and one or two other less famous criminals.*
>
> *The escape was effected by cutting through the ceiling of the cell, which the men were enabled to do so by getting possession of an auger and saw. How they secured these tools is a part of the story which has not yet been explained, and does not matter much to the public since the prisoners are gone and are likely to escape entirely, nothing having been heard of them since they got out.*
>
> *The theory in regard to the escape is that the men after cutting through the wooden ceiling climbed out with the assistance of Thacker, who being a tall man was selected as the one who should push the others up. Thacker was consequently the last man to attempt to get out, and was unable to do so because the other men,*

15

having gotten through the aperture and being themselves free, did not have time to help him in return for his assistance to them.

The shackles of the prisoners were taken off by means of a key and left in the cell. The jailer says that he lost a key some weeks ago and said nothing about having done so because he had several duplicates. All the shackles could be opened by one key and it is presumed that the prisoners must have found the one lost by the jailer.

Thacker says that the reason he did not go too was because he did not want to escape, preferring to stay and stand his trial. This, however, does not possess the requisite amount of thickness, as Thacker's crime was a most revolting one and he stands about as good a chance of swinging as any man in the jail did.

The jail at Los Lunas is built of stone but the ceiling consisted merely of inch boards, to cut through which was no difficult task.

The newspaper did not identify the "euphonious alias" used by one of the escapees. Francisco's two murder victims were identified as brothers, Eutimio (or Ultimio) and Termino Baca, apparently not related to the policeman, both shot during a drunken row in a Belen store.

It might be noted that the Los Lunas jailbreak occurred less than a week after Elfego said that he and Billy the Kid arrived in Albuquerque (the day Yarberry shot Campbell). Furthermore, Elfego claimed that he and Billy "continued to stay around Albuquerque and vicinity perhaps a couple of weeks."

Baca told Crichton that as a young man he received a plea for help from a cousin, Conrado Baca, who, with Frank Shaw, operated a store and saloon in the mining town of Kelly, about twenty-five miles west of Socorro. The two business partners told Baca that a rowdy element, consisting of miners and cowboys, had been staging drunken revels in their emporium on Saturday nights. The carousers typically turned the place into a shooting gallery, using various items of merchandise as targets.

Baca said he went alone to Kelly and, finding the Saturday night spree in progress at the unattended store, calmed the revelers merely by identifying himself as Elfego Baca, a name already gaining respect in the region. The revelers left quietly.

Believing that his cousin and Shaw were unfit to run such a business, Baca took it upon himself to close up shop. He said he sent word to all the Hispanic citizens in the vicinity that he would give away all the merchandise in the store the next day on a first-come, first-served basis. Large crowds assembled at the store to take advantage of the free offer, and the store was soon depleted of all it contained. How the owners reacted to Bacas generous actions was left untold.

Baca also told Crichton that while serving as a Socorro County deputy sheriff he tracked down and captured a murderer at a Sandoval County sheep camp by blackening his skin with burnt cork and posing as the colored servant of his guide, sixteen-year-old Alfredo Montoya of Albuquerque. No time period was given for this episode.

A Fourth of July celebration in the Socorro plaza about 1883. (Courtesy Museum of New Mexico, photo by S.M. Shaw, negative no. 14806).

18

The "Mexican War"

Elfego Baca was nineteen years old in the fall of 1884 when he became involved in what has become known as one of the classic conflicts in the history of the Western frontier, a conflict that pitted a teenaged "Mexican" youth against scores of boisterous "American" cowboys. Ranking in popular imagination alongside the famous gunfight at the O.K. Corral in Tombstone, Arizona, Baca's fight with the Texas cowboys has been the subject of countless articles as well as films and Hispanic folk songs.

The scene of the conflict consisted of three small Hispanic farm villages along a three-mile stretch of the San Francisco River in the extreme western part of Socorro County, near the Arizona border, a remote and rugged region of mountains and pine forests. The three villages were known collectively as San Francisco and individually as the Upper, Middle, and Lower San Francisco Plazas, commonly called the Frisco Plazas.

The upper or northernmost plaza was also known at the time as Milligan's Plaza, as it was here that William R. Milligan, an Army veteran, operated a building containing a general store, a saloon, and living quarters. Later, with the creation of forest reserves in the vicinity, the upper settlement was renamed Reserve, and it is now the seat of Catron County, which was created in 1921 from the western portion of Socorro County.

The Hispanic villagers, who settled there in the 1870s, were joined in the early 1880s by English-speaking neighbors, cattlemen from Texas and elsewhere who drove their herds into the lush valleys and established large ranches on public lands in the vicinity. Cowboys from these ranches flocked to Milligan's Saloon, and after heavy drinking, they often proceeded to celebrate by terrorizing the villagers. The Hispanic farmers in turn angered the cattlemen by impounding livestock that strayed into their gardens and fields and damaged their crops.

It was into this explosive atmosphere that the young Elfego Baca entered to become the central figure in what some referred to, with great exaggeration, as the "Mexican War," October 29–31, 1884.

Several eyewitness versions have been published as to what happened following Baca's arrival at the San Francisco Plazas, and they do not agree on a number of details. This is Baca's version, rather sketchy at times, as he related it in his 1924 pamphlet.

> About the middle of October, 1884, I was working with Jose Baca, big merchant at Socorro. He was paying me $20 a month together with board and room for my services. At that time there was a whole lot of shooting and killing at Socorro, but the worst spot was west of Socorro, called Frisco. Frisco was divided into Upper, Middle and Lower Frisco. We didn't have any newspapers then, there was only a few in the country.
>
> About the middle of October, 1884, a man by the name of Pedro Saraccino, brother-in-law of Jose Baca owner of the store where I was working. He had a big Deputy's badge. He came to talk to me frequently at that time and he told me that while he was Deputy Sheriff at Lower Frisco, because the cowboys at the time

20

were raising all kinds of disturbances. He told me that if he arrested anybody that his life would become thereafter in danger.

He told me that before he left Frisco for Socorro about six or seven cowboys drinking at his own place got hold of a Mexican called "El Burro." They laid him on the counter, one of the boys sat on his chest and arms and the other one on his lap and right there and then the poor Burro was alterated in the presence of everybody.

Then a man by the name of Epitacio Martinez happened to be present, objected and begged them not to do that. The result was that after they finished with Burro, the same cowboys got hold of Epitacio Martinez and measured about twenty or thirty steps from where they were and tied him. Then they used Epitacio as a target and they betted the drinks on who was a better shooter. Martinez was shot four different times. But still he didn't die, he finally died in Gallup about two years ago, he also has a brother by the name of Tomas Martinez who is still living.

I told Saraccino the deputy sheriff that he should be ashamed of himself, having the law on his side to permit the cowboys [to] do what they did. He told me that if I wanted to, I could take his job. I told him that if he would take me back to Frisco with him, that I would make myself a self-made deputy.

We left for Frisco about two or three days after that on a buck-board with a big mule. Half of the time we had to help the mule climb every steep hill. When in Frisco he took me to his house. I was expecting to run up against anything any minute.

Three days after we arrived there we went over to what is called the Upper Plaza or Milligan's Plaza. Milligan was the owner of a big store together with Whiskey Bar where the cowboys had [a] lot of fun. I was talking to the Justice of the Peace of that precinct named Lopez, when here comes a couple of cowboys shooting up the town. Afterwards they went into Milligan's place where there was plenty of cowboys drinking. I told the J.P. why that should be allowed there. The judge told me that it couldn't be stopped because the Slaughter's Outfit had about 150 cowboys. When a bunch of them came into town, they shot dogs, chickens, cats, etc.

Just then I saw a cowboy butt another on the head about two or three times. I walked up to the fellow using the gun and he had already fired five shots. I commanded him to quit that I was a self-made deputy in order to keep order. He turned around and shot my hat off. That started the rest of the performances.

He got away from me and I went over to the ranch where he was working. He got out of the ranch through the back door. There must have been about thirty cowboys. I only had one man with me by the name of Francisquito Naranjo, a very brave man. Then I put this cowboy under arrest and took him to Lower Frisco where deputy Saraccino was living.

That night twelve cowboys demanded the release of the man I had under arrest. They were armed to the teeth. I told them that instead of releasing the prisoner I was going to give them time enough to count from one to three before I shoot. They undertook to draw their weapons, then I started "one, two, three" and fired.

When I fired they ran. I killed one man and horse on the run. I hung on to my supposed prisoner.

Next morning about 8:00 o'clock there was two men on horseback that I knew, one of them by the name of Clemente Hightower and Gyrone Martin, they stood about two hundred yards away from me. I commenced to play with my two guns in their direction and they made me a proposition to take the prisoner up to the Upper Frisco. I told them I would do it and that I was coming up single-handed.

I was informed already that there was about one hundred men in the canyon waiting for me to go by there. I went and got almost everybody in the small settlement. Told all the children and women who didn't want their lives in jeopardy to get into the church. When I left there must have been about one hundred and twenty-five people in church.

When I came to the Upper Frisco I talked to the Justice of the Peace and while I was talking to the Justice of the Peace here comes a big bunch of cowboys. The testimony in court showed that there must have been about eighty cowboys. I knew two of the cowboys and I walked up to them and threw their guns on the ground. By that time I saw another man by the name of Wilson. I said "Hello, Mr. Wilson," his answer was "Hello, you little Mexican, etc., etc."

By that time a man behind him fired a shot at me. I don't think he intended to shoot me because there was some more of his people in back of me. I drew my guns and backed up to a picket house called "Hakal" [jacal] belonging to a man by the name of Geronimo Armijo. Molo Armijo his son who must have been about eight

23

years old now living in Magdalena was on the roof, the so-called "Hackal" [sic] husking corn. He and another boy went down in a hurry.

I went into the house and put the lady and children out, then the fight started. One man got off his horse in a hurry by the name of Kearns, he said "I'll get that little Mexican out of there." I could see him when he got off his horse through the cracks of the door. I shot at him with both guns at the same time.

A man by the name of Jim Cook was leading the fight against me. He is now in Nebraska. He was in charge of Slaughter's Outfit. That started the fight well and good. I was hungry while I was there, but I found some beef and made beef-stew, coffee and tortillas. The court evidence shows that over four hundred shots were fired at me within thirty-six hours. At the Hackal the only big objects were Nuestra Senora Santa Ana, a statue believed to be over six hundred years old. And neither the statue nor I was hit.

Finally a deputy sheriff by the name of Ross showed up there, a deputy whom I knew at Socorro. He and Jim Cook asked me to surrender. I told deputy Ross, I am your prisoner but I will not surrender my guns. We went into an understanding with Mr. Ross and Mr. Cook. That Mr. Ross was to have six cowboys from Frisco to Socorro about one hundred and sixty-five miles but the guards should be at least thirty long spaces or steps ahead of me. They were to ride horseback and I was to be behind with Mr. Ross on a buckboard.

At that time they were building a jail in Socorro and I was put in it while they were putting the roof on it. The place where they put me was a cell about four feet square with two iron doors. They kept me there for four months, then brought me to Albuquerque for my first trial on a change of venue. When they brought me to Albuquerque they put two pairs of handcuffs, one pair welded by a blacksmith, and also two pairs of shackles for my legs.

When they arrived with me in Albuquerque the first thing the Albuquerque sheriff did was to take me to a blacksmith to take off the hand-cuffs. I was tried for murder and found innocent. From then on I made up my mind, I wanted the outlaws to hear my steps a block away from me. I have always been for law and order and I will be till I die. Since that time I wanted to be an "A No.-1" peace officer, likewise a criminal lawyer.

Baca's account, as far as it went, was a fairly accurate recital of his role in the three-day conflict, but it did contain a number of errors, due perhaps to his fading memory forty years after the event. Fortunately, additional details of the dramatic episode are revealed in a number of eye-witness and newspaper accounts.

The Jim Cook whom Baca referred to in his narrative was James H. Cook, manager of the WS Ranch at Alma, about thirty miles south of the San Francisco Plazas. Cook published his version of the Baca fight in *Fifty Years on the Old Frontier*, first published in 1923. Crichton, in his 1928 biography of Baca, relied heavily on Cook's version, interrupting it at intervals with Baca's comments.

William French, who succeeded Cook as manager of the WS Ranch, published his eyewitness version in *Some Recollections of a Western Ranchman*, first published in 1928.

25

Elfego Baca at about the time of his battle with the cowboys. (Courtesy Museum of New Mexico, negative no. 75265).

Both Cook and French identified Baca as a deputy sheriff, and both said he was visiting small settlements in the county campaigning for the reelection of Socorro County Sheriff Pedro (Pete) Simpson when he arrived at the Frisco Plazas. Baca said nothing about an electioneering trip, however.

The man Baca arrested at Milligan's Plaza was Charlie McCarty, his surname often given as McCarthy, a twenty-two-year-old cowboy employed by John B. Slaughter, who had arrived in the vicinity in 1883 from Texas with large numbers of cattle and cowboys, although not nearly the one hundred and fifty cowboys mentioned in Baca's narrative. John B. Slaughter should not be confused with John H. Slaughter, another Texas cattleman who became a noted sheriff of Cochise County, Arizona.

Patrocinio Martinez, a pioneer Socorro County rancher, recalled in a 1958 interview that he was a boy of eleven or twelve years of age when Baca made his appearance at the San Francisco Plazas. At the time, he said, a group of farmers had gathered at the home of his uncle, Espiridion Armijo, at the Lower Plaza to help with the harvesting and that he was staying at his uncle's home and working as a water boy for the harvesters. Shortly before noon one day, Martinez said, a young man arrived at his uncle's home in a one-horse buggy and identified himself as Elfego Baca, a deputy sheriff.

"None of us believed him at first," Martinez said. "One of the women laughed and said he was too young to be a deputy sheriff."

According to Martinez, Baca produced some papers that he said proved his identity, and then he told the farmers he needed some help to arrest a cowboy named

Charlie McCarty. Some of the farmers agreed to help Baca but first invited him to sit down and eat dinner with them, which he did.

Five of the farmers offered to assist Baca in making the arrest, Martinez said, and accompanied him to the Upper Plaza after dinner. Martinez identified the five as Francisco Martinez, Jose Andres Montoya, Patrocinio Romero, Jose T. Montoya, and his uncle. He said Baca and his five companions arrested McCarty and took him to a house at the Middle Plaza for safekeeping, as there was no jail in the vicinity.

"Gabriel Taylor, a colored man, was ordered to guard the prisoner in the house overnight, and Baca spent the night at my uncle's house," Martinez said. "The prisoner got away during the night, but Baca did not know it until the next day."

Baca had decided to arrest McCarty after seeing him firing his revolver in Milligan's establishment and out in the street. He asked a justice of the peace why he allowed a cowboy to jeopardize life and property in such a way, and the justice replied that if the cowboy were arrested or harmed, his friends would come to town and do a lot of harm. Baca told the justice that he would show McCarty that "there was at least one Mexican in the county who was not afraid of an American cowboy."

Cook wrote that McCarty "was not really a bad man, merely a little too playful at times," and French called McCarty "an inoffensive youth incapable of harming an insect." Baca and his companions disarmed McCarty, and when the justice of the peace refused to try him, Baca said he would take McCarty to Socorro for trial. In the meantime, McCarty was taken to a house on the

Middle Plaza and placed under guard.

Milligan, who at first demanded McCarty's arrest, changed his mind after the arrest was made, fearing retaliation by McCarty's cowboy friends, who patronized his business. Learning that McCarty was being held prisoner in a house at the Middle Plaza, a group of Slaughter's cowboys, accompanied by Milligan, rode to the house and demanded his release. The group was led by Slaughter's ranch foreman, Young Parham, his surname also given as Perham, Purham, and Perryman, among others.

Parham and his companions demanded McCarty's release, and after some futile discussion, Baca gave them to the count of three to leave, and he and his companions opened fire, which was returned by the cowboys in a mad scramble for safety. In the brief exchange, the horse Parham was riding was hit and fell over on its rider, causing injuries to the ranch foreman that were to prove fatal. Another cowboy, Tabe Allen, received a bullet in the knee. The cowboys fled the scene.

In the tradition of Paul Revere, cowboy couriers rode swiftly to cattle ranches in the region that afternoon, claiming with great exaggeration that the Mexicans at the San Francisco Plazas had gone on the warpath, had killed four or five men, and were threatening to kill all Americans in the vicinity. Alarmed cowboys from the various ranches quickly saddled their horses and sped to the scene of the supposed conflict.

There were no newspapers in that part of Socorro County at the time, and rumors of the conflict soon spread over the territory. At Silver City, about one hundred miles to the south, the weekly newspaper *Southwest Sentinel* published this report on November 1:

A rumor brought by Mr. Graham comes to us that a fight has occurred close to American valley between Mexicans and stockmen. On Wednesday (October 29) a courier came into Alma and asked for a relief party, telling of the fight and saying four or five men had been killed, among whom was John Slaughter's foreman. An armed party of twenty men left Alma Wednesday evening at 7 o'clock for the scene of the conflict, since which time nothing has been heard from them up to the time Mr. Graham left Alma.

The Black Range, a weekly newspaper in the mining town of Chloride, about seventy miles southeast of the San Francisco Plazas, published a report of the conflict on November 14 that referred to Parham as Perryman and mistakenly placed Milligan's store at the Middle Plaza. According to the article:

Mr. Broiles, foreman of the Gila cattle company, was at the scene of the trouble a few days thereafter, and the story he heard is as follows:

Young Perryman, John Slaughter's foreman, was at Milligan's store in Middle Plaza with two of his men on the day when the difficulty began, and the two men getting filled with poor whiskey had a quarrel between themselves.

This was amicably settled, however, and peace was resumed, but one of them had not yet put aside his revolver when it was accidentally discharged. The shot did no damage, but the noise aroused Deputy Sheriff Baca, who came to the store and made the arrest of the author

of the report and took him to his house for safe keeping.
*Perryman, after some time, went to Baca and
asked that his man be tried, fined and set at liberty at
once, as he needed his services, but his request was
refused, and it is claimed that with few more words fire
was opened on Perryman from a dozen or more guns
which constitued Baca's guard. Perryman, who was
on horseback, wheeled and fled when the shooting began, and although the range was short and the shots
not less than fifty, not a bullet struck him. His horse,
however, was killed under him, and the animal falling
to the side on which he was leaning struck the ground
with his rider underneath, crushing Perryman so badly
that at last accounts his life was despaired of. He was
unconscious when Mr. Broiles saw him several days
after the injury.*

*This action was considered an outrage by the
cattlemen, aroused their ire, and they resolved that
Baca should be arrested.*

By the next morning, October 30, scores of cowboys
from neighboring ranches had converged on the Upper
Plaza, the newcomers including both Cook and French,
Deputy Sheriff Dan Bechdolt of Alma, and a justice of the
peace from outside the community. Not finding any
"Mexican War" in progress, as they had been led to believe, most of them entered Milligan's and began drinking
at the bar. Cook estimated that there were eighty cowboys
gathered in the community that morning.

A small delegation proceeded to the house at the
Middle Plaza where Baca and his friends were holding

McCarty prisoner and entered into a signed agreement with Baca that he would not be harmed if he delivered his prisoner to the Upper Plaza at a certain hour for trial before a justice of the peace. Baca, accompanied by several of his friends and the prisoner, rode to the Upper Plaza at the appointed hour, dismounted in front of Milligan's, and walked fifty or sixty yards south to a home where the court session was to be held. Cowboys streamed out of Milligan's and followed them down the road, one of them, Sam Wilson, cursing Baca along the way.

After a brief hearing, McCarty was found guilty of drunk and disorderly conduct and was fined five dollars, which he paid. He complained that Baca still had his gun, taken from him when he was disarmed. But Baca had disappeared.

Baca, the first to leave the courtroom, strode out the door to find a large group of angry cowboys milling around outside. Pulling his hat down over his eyes, he disappeared around a corner of the building and walked hurriedly down a back lane to the small home of Geronimo Armijo, which stood in a clearing. Seeking refuge in the house, he advised Mrs. Armijo to leave in a hurry. Upon leaving, she padlocked the only door to the house from the outside.

The Armijo house, which Baca referred to in his writing as a "Hakal," was of the type known in the Spanish language as a *jacal*, a flimsy structure with thin walls consisting of upright poles or slabs plastered over inside and out with mud, supporting a dirt covered roof. The dirt floor was twelve or eighteen inches below ground level, a feature Baca soon was to find quite useful.

The cowboys headed back to Milligan's for a few

more drinks before departing for their various ranches. Several of them approached French and asked him if he knew where Baca had gone, and French pointed to the Armijo house down the road. One of the cowboys, William B. "Bert" Hearne, of the nearby Spur Ranch, told French that the judge had given him authority to arrest Baca in connection with the shootings the previous day at the Middle Plaza, when Parham had been seriously injured and Allen wounded. Hearne, referred to as Kearns by Baca, was identified as Hern, Herne, and Heron in other accounts.

French wrote that he accompanied Hearne and several other cowboys to the house, that Hearne knocked on the door and asked if anybody was inside, and that, receiving no answer, he began kicking on the door violently, reportedly exclaiming, "I'll get that little Mexican out of there!" Two bullets, fired from inside the house, crashed through the thin door, one of them hitting Hearne in the abdomen. He cursed and fell unconscious into French's arms.

French and several other cowboys dragged the wounded man to safety, around the corner of the house, and when he regained consciousness, they placed him on a horse and led him to Milligan's, where his wound was washed and dressed. The bullet wound proved fatal, however, French writing that Hearne "petered out" during the night.

Some of the cowboys, including Cook, had already left the village when Baca fired through the door of the house, and, hearing the shots, they hurried back to the Upper Plaza. Cook wrote that some of Baca's Mexican friends had gathered in the hills overlooking the plaza, and it was feared they were attacking the Americans in the village. Learning upon their return that Hearne had been shot while attempting to gain entry to the house in which Baca had taken refuge, an estimated forty-five to sixty cowboys began taking up positions surrounding the house. Baca, shooting through cracks in the picket walls, began drilling holes in the tall hats of those who approached too close for comfort. The cowboys opened a fusillade on the house, the bullets crashing through the thin walls, shattering the wood and mud plaster, and damaging almost everything in the house except Baca, who kept shooting at his attackers from a prone position on the floor.

French and some of his friends took positions behind the buttresses of an adobe church on the opposite side of the street from the house and began exchanging shots with Baca, whose bullets knocked chunks out of the adobe walls. Some of the cowboys concealed themselves behind blankets they stretched between nearby houses, facing Baca's fire each time they exposed themselves. One cowboy approached the house shielding himself behind what had been the cast-iron front of a stove but beat a hasty retreat when Baca creased his scalp with a bullet. The one-sided battle continued until nightfall, when the attackers retired from the scene, leaving a few sentries to watch the house.

Baca told Crichton that the cowboys dynamited the house during the night, causing a section of it to collapse, but this is doubtful, although attempts were made to set the house on fire. Cook wrote that a party was dispatched to the Cooney mining camp near Alma to get some dynamite with which to blow up the house but made no mention of dynamite arriving or being used. French wrote that blazing logs were hurled onto the roof of the house in a futile effort to burn it down. Patrocinio Martinez said in his 1958 interview that no dynamite was used but that the cowboys got some rags at Milligan's store, soaked them in kerosene, ignited them, and threw them at the house, setting a small fire. One section of the dirt roof reportedly collapsed when a wall, weakened by bullet holes, gave way.

Weary cowboys returned to the battleground in the morning, convinced that Baca could not have survived the barrage of bullets that had penetrated all sides of the flimsy *jacal*. To their surprise, they found that the besieged man was very much alive and was calmly preparing a breakfast of hot coffee and tortillas inside the house. Once again, they opened fire on the house, the barrage continuing at intervals throughout the day.

Late that afternoon, Frank Rose, a Socorro County deputy sheriff, arrived on the scene, and he agreed to take custody of Baca and escort him to Socorro for trial if he could be persuaded to surrender. Cook and an interpreter, Francisquito (or Francisco) Naranjo, approached the *jacal* and called on Baca to surrender, Cook saying he would be responsible for his life if Baca would agree to surrender and be taken to Socorro for trial. Naranjo repeated the surrender offer in Spanish.

Baca, agreeing to the surrender terms, scrambled out through a small window of the house, coatless, with a six-shooter in each hand, looking suspiciously about him as if fearing treachery. Cook wrote that the cowboys, who had their rifles trained on Baca, wanted to hang him at once but that he dissuaded them from their intentions by teiling them that they constituted a mob in the eyes of the law and that Baca undoubtedly would be tried and legally hanged. Baca's Prince Albert coat was secured for him, and he turned himself over to Deputy Sheriff Rose on the condition that he keep his own gun.

Cook wrote that four thousand shots had been fired into the small house during the thirty-three-hour siege, reducing practically every household item to splinters. Untouched, however, was a life-sized statue of a saint, Nuestra Senora Santa Ana, which Baca came to regard as his guardian angel during his long ordeal.

Baca, who originally had said that four hundred shots were fired into the house, later adopted Cook's much higher figure. Rancher Montague Stevens, who was there, said in a 1953 interview that the four thousand figure was much too high, adding that ammunition was scarce at the time and that he doubted if there were four thousand rounds of ammunition in all of Socorro County in 1884.

Baca was escorted to Socorro in a buckboard, his captors apparently agreeing to his terms—that he be allowed to remain armed and that the guards should ride in front of him. He was jailed in Socorro to await grand jury action in connection with the killing of Hearne.

Although Baca claimed late in his life that he killed four cowboys and wounded eight others during the affray at the Frisco Plazas, the evidence shows that the only man he actually killed was William Hearne. The only other casualties were Young Parham, who died of injuries suffered when his horse fell on him, and Tabe Allen, who was shot in the knee at the same time, during an exchange of gunfire between two armed parties. Neither French nor

Cook mentioned any other casualties.

The *Silver City Enterprise* reported a week later, on November 7, that "there were no other casualties," and the *Albuquerque Evening Democrat* published this brief item on November 18: "True to its history, Socorro County has another bloody tragedy at the Mogollons. A cowboy named Heron was killed by Deputy Sheriff Baca and another man was wounded."

The fact that only one cowboy was shot during the long siege at the *jacal* indicates that Baca, who was considered a good shot, was shooting not to kill but only to keep his attackers at bay. Also, the length of Baca's ordeal at the Frisco Plazas might be attributed to the fact that most of the verbal and written communications directed to him were in the Spanish language, of which he had only a limited knowledge at the time.

The Murder Trial

A Socorro County grand jury returned an indictment charging Elfego Baca with the murder of William B. Hearne, and the trial, moved to Bernalillo County on a change of venue, opened in Albuquerque on May 7, 1885, District Judge William H. Brinker presiding. The prosecuting attorneys for the Territory of New Mexico were C. C. McComas and Neill B. Field, and Baca's defense attorneys were Judge John W. Shaw and H. B. Hamilton of Socorro and Pearce S. Rodey of Albuquerque.

The trial was held in an adobe courthouse just east of Albuquerque's Old Town Plaza.

The *Albuquerque Evening Democrat*, the only newspaper that provided a running account of the three-day trial, published some of the testimony, probably condensed, and sometimes confusing, as the witnesses undoubtedly were responding to questions that were not included in the articles. As was a common practice among New Mexico newspapers at the time, names of persons often were spelled phonetically. The name of the victim, William Hearne, appeared in the articles as both William Herne and Burt Hurn. He apparently was known to his friends as Burt, or Bert, Hearne. Charlie McCarty's surname was given as McCarthy in all the newspaper references to him, and the original spellings will be maintained in the newspaper excerpts presented below.

The *Democrat* reported that Judge Shaw, a Socorro

lawyer and evangelist, said in his opening statement for the defense "that Baca was sheriff at San Francisco, that he had arrested McCarthy for discharging his pistol in the city limits, his cowboy friends went to town in full force and threatened to kill the sheriff and wipe out the town, that Baca in order to keep from being killed went to another house, and that if he did shoot the man, it was perfectly justifiable." The newspaper added, "Taken in all, the judge made a very clear and concise statement and the opinion is that Baca will be released."

Among defense exhibits entered into evidence was a deputy sheriff's commission, signed by Socorro County Sheriff Pedro A. Simpson, issued to Elfego Baca, dated October 26, 1884, a few days before Baca arrived at the San Francisco Plazas. Unless this document was fraudulent, Baca was not a "self-appointed" deputy as he later was to claim.

The newspaper reported that Charles McCarthy (McCarty) was the first prosecution witness to testify at the trial but that his testimony was not available as there was no newspaper reporter in court at the time.

James Wadsworth, identified as the second prosecution witness, testified that he was at the office of the justice of the peace at the Upper Plaza on October 30, 1884, when a large group of armed cowboys from John Slaughter's ranch rode up. He said Baca had filed a complaint against McCarthy charging McCarthy with trying to murder him and had sent a man to the Middle Plaza for witnesses. Wadsworth said that, as the armed cowboys were approaching, McCarthy remarked, "Look at the crowd of men coming here." Wadsworth continued:

As soon as he saw the men coming Baca stepped out of the back door and that was the last seen of him. The men rode up and got off their horses, and walked into the justice's office. They remained there about an hour. They waited for Baca to come back, but he came not.

Some of the boys went out to hunt Baca. McCarthy wanted his pistol, which Baca had. I got the keys to his house and with several others went there [and] tried to unlock the door. One of the men said the door was not locked, and Burt Hurn [sic] tried to unlock the door. As he pushed on the door two shots were fired by someone in the house, and Burt staggered back and said, "Boys, I'm killed."

There were about eight or nine men in the crowd that went to the house. Hurn staggered off about twenty feet and fell; he got over the fence and fell again; when he fell the last time two of the men ran to where he was and picked him up and carried him into Milligan's store, where he died in about an hour.

During cross-examination, Wadsworth testified that he and his eight or nine companions did not enter the house and did not see who was inside. He said the men had pistols in their scabbards (holsters), that four or five had rifles, and that Baca had two .45-caliber pistols when he left the justice's office.

O. B. Bishop testified for the prosecution that he was among the men who went to the house, that someone pushed on the door on the east side of the house, and that Hearne was killed when two shots were fired from inside the house. Nothing was said from inside the house prior to the shooting, he said, and he did not hear anyone say they would kill the defendant, adding that he heard everything that was said.

A. M. Loftus testified for the prosecution that he was among the men who went to the house, that he did not hear any insulting or threatening language as they approached the house, and that nobody said anything about killing Baca. During cross-examination, he admitted that there was "a lot of loud talk."

The newspaper reported that testimony was taken from several other prosecution witnesses "and that all told nearly the same story."

According to Crichton's biography of Baca, one cowboy testified at the trial that if he took a .45 Colt pistol, aimed it directly at Baca's chest from a foot away, and fired, there would be absolutely no effect, as he believed that Baca was possessed of something from God or the devil. Baca also told Crichton that exhibits at the trial included the door of the *jacal*, which contained 367 bullet holes, and a broom with eight bullet holes in the handle. The newspaper made no mention of any such testimony or exhibits.

The only defense testimony published by the *Democrat* was that of the defendant, Elfego Baca, who agreed to testify in his own behalf. The testimony of the twenty-year-old defendant, as published in the newspaper, differs in some respects from the version he published forty years later in his political pamphlet. The newspaper omitted the questions he was answering and may have condensed his testimony, since parts of his courtroom narrative do not seem to be in chronological order and there appear to be a number of contradictions.

This is Baca's testimony as it appeared in the Albuquerque newspaper on May 9, 1885:

*On the morning of the 28th of October I was
called on to arrest a man for firing a revolver in Milligan's house, and started out immediately to do my duty.
I arrested him in the upper precinct, but as there was
no justice of the peace there to try him, I took him to the
middle precinct, or plaza.*

*At 2 o'clock I was at Milligan's and McCarthy,
my prisoner, commenced firing off his revolver at everything and everybody. Milligan went out yelling, he
knew I was a deputy sheriff, and asked me to help him.
When I asked McCarthy to stop he had fired five shots,
and instead of stopping he fired the last of the five shots
at me. I went home and got some men to help me arrest
him, because I had no arms at the time.*

*I got eight or nine men and went back to Milli-
gan's house and did not find McCarthy there. I went to
a ranch two or three hundred yards away and again did
not find him, but when coming back I met him on the
road. He started to run and I asked one of my deputies
who it was that was running, and he said it was
McCarthy. Then I had the guards to arrest him. All the
way up to jail he abused me in a very insulting manner,
stopping every minute or so, and crying he did not need
to be taken and wouldn't have to go if he didn't want
to. He was very drunk.*

*At the Upper Plaza, a large number of cowboys had
assembled, and as there was no justice there, I took him
down to the Middle Plaza. He drew Parham's pistol and shot
it at me. Then I refused to let him off or have any bail.*

Sararcino and Parham were willing to be his bondsmen, and at first I concluded to let him out on bail, and had three or four lines of bond written when Milligan came in, very drunk and insulting. He rapped on the counter and said that no bond should be allowed in McCarthy's case. I then had the prisoner placed in a house and guarded.

When Milligan went out he told McCarthy he would return soon enough with men to rescue him. He returned in about two hours to take McCarthy out, and said he was strong and big enough to take him out. I ordered the boys after he went away that if I was not there when Milligan returned, not to let him approach the place.

When he came back it was about two or three hours afterward. I told him to stop, as I was present at the time. He said that he would not stop, that he wanted Charlie McCarthy. I told him that it did not make any difference, that I had McCarthy in charge. He said that didn't make any difference as he had arms to rescue the prisoner with.

It was reported that there was a large number of cowboys in town. I told Milligan to go away. He would not go. I then drew a pistol and fired a shot into the ground to see if he would go. He said: "You are a bad shot, you didn't hit me." I told him that I didn't want to shoot anybody, and that I wanted him to go away. He said he would go away and started to go where his horses were hitched. He returned soon and talked very insultingly. I told him to go away, that he was making me tired. Then he mounted his horse, and again dismounted, came back and said, "The devil may take me if I don't get Charlie McCarthy out." I then ordered the guards to fire, and the two discharges went off about the same time — their fire and our fire.

I did not take McCarthy up to a justice's office the next day at 9 o'clock as I had intended. At about 10 o'clock he made his escape. We went after him and overtook him near Milligan's house. I again put him under arrest.

On the 30th a large number of cowboys came to town from their ranches. They asked me why I didn't give him an examination. I told them I didn't know what to do with him, that I knew that there were men waiting for me in the upper precinct. They signed an agreement with me that I should not be molested that day.

The guards would not go with me to the Upper Plaza because they were afraid of the people up there. I finally got Jose Montoya and others to go. They promised me they would not hurt the guards or me. I stopped with the prisoner, and two Texans, when about half way up there, one went on one side of the road, and the other kept on. Then I went to the courtroom and commenced to make out a list of witnesses. J. Parpzia was told to go and get them, but before he went we saw a lot of men coming; they were all armed, carried their arms in their hands.

Geronimo [Armijo] then spoke to [Sam] Wilson and released him, then Wilson talked very insultingly to me, and said he didn't want to talk to me. I then drew my pistol and told him that I did not want to talk to him, either, then I went out in the direction of Geronimo's house. I watched to see if anyone was following me.

I entered the house and the woman locked the door and went away, I don't know where. I heard several *men around the house. I heard their talk and they wanted to kill me. One of them said in English that it was just a padlock that fastened the door, and they had better go and get a key.*

They went away, and returned in a few minutes and pushed the door. They again went around the house. One of them said this door is not locked. He shoved the door at one of the middle rooms. The others were trying to unlock the door. I remained where I was. They pushed on the door but did not open it. When they did open the door, they all said "let us fire." They commenced firing through all the doors, and I fired a few shots through the windows, then they pushed the door again, and I fired two shots through the door. This is all I know.

I was not acquainted with Mr. William Herne, the man killed. Never had anything to do with him.

I saw them at Armijo's house. There were about 10 or 11 of them present; saw them through the window; some had rifles and all had pistols. Heard them talking outside. They had their weapons in their hands. They came to the house with pistols and said they would get me out.

The newspaper said Baca gave these answers to questions asked during his cross-examination:

There was only one door and one window in the house where I was. They came up to the house from an easterly direction. They rode around the house.

I did fire two shots through the door when one of them said he would get me out. No shots were fired previous.

The men came to the door only once. Some of them made a proposition to get some keys and get into the house. They tried to open the door when they came back. They were gone about four or five minutes. Some were on foot and others on horseback.

I do not know Loftus. I recognize him as the man who brought me from San Francisco [Plaza], but don't know his name.

I am not acquainted with Frank Rose. He was a deputy sheriff and I gave myself up to him.

On the way to Socorro we overtook a team and wagon containing a coffin. I did not ask who was in the coffin for the reason I thought I might be in one myself soon.

The jury, after a short deliberation, returned a not guilty verdict. The newspaper identified the jurors, all Bernalillo County residents, as Demetrio Garcia, Ramon Martin, Elisio Gutierrez, Soto Armijo, Cecilio Garcia, Jesus Perea, Thomas Garcia y Montoya, Juan Gutierres, Andres Lucero, Felipe Garcia, Juan C. Griegos, and Juan Garcia y Rael.

In another trial, a Socorro County jury tried and acquitted Baca and a number of his friends of a murder charge brought in connection with the death of Young Parham (referred to on at least one court document as William Young Pashaw), who died of injuries suffered when his horse was shot and fell on him during the exchange of gunfire at the Middle Plaza.

The jubilant Baca now had achieved the reputation of a "tough hombre" that he was to put to good use for the remainder of his long life.

Both Jailer and Prisoner

hile standing trial in Albuquerque's Old Town, Baca met and became acquainted with sixteen-year-old Francisquita Pohmer, a student at Sister Blandina's School in Old Town and the daughter of Joseph and Dolores Chavez Pohmer of Albuquerque. Elfego proposed marriage to Francisquita, and she promised to marry him if he was acquitted of the murder charges against him. Despite the objections of her father, a native of Germany who owned an Old Town meat market, she and Baca were married on August 13, 1885.

The young couple took up residence in Albuquerque, Baca writing later that he was a Bernalillo County deputy sheriff and county jailer at the time, serving until the winter of 1886–87, when he was appointed a deputy United States marshal. If Baca was a deputy sheriff in Albuquerque in the 1880s, it apparently was not common knowledge, for the local newspapers, in reporting some of his minor scrapes with the law, sometimes referred to him as "an Old Town Mexican" and "a ruffian."

The *Albuquerque Journal*, which usually spelled his given name as Elfigo, published this brief article on August 15, 1886:

> *Elfigo Baca, an old town Mexican, was arraigned before Judge [W. C.] Heacock yesterday on a charge of displaying a deadly weapon in a threatening manner. Upon the charge he was fined $25 and fifty days in the county jail, a decision from which he appealed and gave*

47

$500 bail for fine, costs and appearance. He was tried
on a peace warrant and obliged to give $250 bonds to
keep the peace for one year.

Baca, who was charged specifically with drawing a
pistol on Mrs. Josefa Werner, the complaint brought by
Thomas Werner, stated to the newspaper that the charges
stemmed from a dispute over rental of a piano and that
Taise Pais and another man had threatened to kill him.
The *Journal*, on August 18, published this item:

> *Taise Pais, a resident of Old Town, was arraigned*
> *before Judge Oakes on a charge of assault and battery*
> *on the person of Elfigo Baca, but as the assault was*
> *only a little one the fine was only assessed at $1 and*
> *costs.*

A month later, on August 14, 1886, Baca was accused
of precipitating a near riot on First Street in Albuquerque's
downtown section when he attacked an Albuquerque
police officer in an effort to release a friend whom the
officer had just arrested. The details were published in
The *Albuquerque Journal* the next day under the front-page
headline "Almost a Riot."

According to the newspaper article, the altercation
began in a Negro saloon on First Street when a blacksmith
named Kelly, ordinarily peaceable, made a remark to
Jesus Romero of Old Town, who was playing poker at the
time, which resulted in a fight. E. D. Henry, Albuquerque's assistant town marshal, appeared and arrested both
combatants. Romero resisted arrest, the article said, while
Kelly, who was well known and who volunteered to

appear in court whenever wanted, was released by Henry so that he could devote his entire attention to the struggling Romero. The article continued:

Elfigo Baca, a notorious ruffian, appeared on the scene as a champion of Romero and attempted to take him away from the officer, who in consequence was forced to use his "billy," and after knocking Romero down handcuffed him, thus enabling him to defend himself for the attack of Baca.

Mr. Henry now took his prisoner as far as D. Favor's store, where we regret to say, Sheriff [Santiago] Baca, Francisco Armijo, Captain Martinez and other prominent citizens of the old town, and ordinarily good citizens, appeared on the scene, Sheriff Baca crying in Mexican, "Come on, boys," and made a dash at Officer Henry, who, after a gallant fight for his prisoner, was forced by superior numbers to give him up for a moment, but a moment only.

As soon as Sheriff Baca obtained possession of the prisoner he hurried him away to a street car which was conveniently near, but before he reached it a large crowd of citizens, including several of our best businessmen, rallied to the support of Officer Henry, and he with commendable pluck grabbed his prisoner but not until he had reached the car.

Had it not been for the interference of the crowd the car would have taken the prisoner to the old town, but its wheels were blocked, its horses taken by the bits, and the driver warned by arguments that could not be misunderstood that he could not [leave], neither did he leave. Sheriff Baca, seeing the disposition that now

49

surrounded the car, made a virtue of necessity, and bringing his prisoner out turned him over to Officer Henry, claiming that he wanted to assist him in the arrest.

During the fuss before Dr. Favor's store, Judge Heacock, who saw the affray, ran to Marshal [Michael Robert] McGuire's room, awakened him, and he now arrived and assisted Officer Henry in conveying the prisoner to the lock up from which he was released on $100 bond at a later hour.

The scene during these occurrences beggars description, the street for more than a block being densely packed with excited men, and had an unadvised shot been fired a riot of formidable dimensions and probably serious in its results would have inevitable [sic] ensued.

The whole trouble was precipitated by Elfigo Baca, a man who has twice been acquitted of the charge of murder and who has few friends among either respectable Americans or Mexicans in the territory. Later in the evening, Elfigo Baca, Francisco Armijo and several others were arrested for interfering with an officer, and if the law takes its course other arrests will follow.

Santiago Baca, the Bernalillo County sheriff, told the newspaper the next day that he had made no attempt to take the prisoner away from Officer Henry, that he was only trying to assist him, and that his whole purpose was to prevent a riot.

The newspaper reported on September 21 that Judge Heacock had fined Elfego Baca $15 and costs and Jesus Romero $2 and costs in connection with the affray.

Years later, Baca often boasted that Judge Heacock had ordered him to pay a fine of $10 and costs or serve a thirty-day jail sentence and that since the judge did not know that he was the county jailer in Old Town, he opted for the jail sentence and was escorted to the jail. As the jailer, he said, he was given seventy-five cents a day to feed each prisoner, and as a "prisoner," he received seventy-five cents a day to feed himself, earning him an extra $22.50 during his supposed incarceration.

Baca also said later that he was jailed for slamming the police officer in the head with his large, silver pocket watch. According to the 1886 newspapers, however, it was in connection with the earlier charge of displaying a deadly weapon in a threatening manner that Judge Heacock gave Baca a jail sentence, not in connection with his actions in assaulting the police officer.

Two months later, on November 20, 1886, Marshal Michael Robert "Bob" McGuire and his assistant, E. D. Henry, received word that two cowboy desperadoes for whom they had warrants, Charlie Ross and John "Kid" Johnson, had been seen loitering around Pasqual Cutinola's dance hall in Martineztown, on Albuquerque's north side.

Arriving at the dance hall at 8:30 that evening and finding no trace of the two desperadoes, McGuire and Henry started searching the neighborhood. Looking through the window of a small adobe home about twenty feet south of the dance hall, they saw Ross and Johnson just finishing supper inside with two young women, Simona Moya and Terecita Trujillo. The two officers went to the front door, drew their guns, and started to rush in the door just as Simona Moya, holding an empty pitcher, started out the door to get some water from a well. All went down in a heap.

McGuire jumped back up, rushed to one side of the room where Kid Johnson was sitting on a trunk, and attempted to disarm him. Henry, his progress blocked momentarily by the half opened door, charged toward Ross, who was sitting on a bed.

Ross, who had drawn his gun during the scramble at the doorway, downed Henry with a bullet in the leg. The lights went out, but the shooting continued, the two young women diving under the bed. When the shooting stopped, Ross and Johnson ran out the door and disappeared in the darkness.

Officer Henry was dead on the floor of the smoke-filled room with two bullets in his chest and one in his leg. Marshal McGuire also was down, still alive, but with two bullets in his side and one in his arm. His wounds were to prove fatal.

The wounded Ross was found and arrested the next morning in a house near the scene of the gun battle and was taken to the Bernalillo County Jail in Old Town. No trace was found of Johnson, described by the *Albuquerque Daily Democrat* as "full of cowboy swagger, wears a Chihuahua hat and wears his pants in his boots."

McGuire lingered until November 26 before dying of his wounds, at which time flags in Albuquerque were lowered to half-staff and black mourning crepe placed on business houses. His remains were taken to his hometown of Oswego, New York, for burial. Henry, an Ohio native, was buried in Albuquerque's Fairview Cemetery.

Charlie Ross remained in the county jail until the night of January 3, 1887, when he and another prisoner,

Peter Trinkaus of Gallup, who had been convicted of murder, escaped through an unbarred window after opening their cell with a key they had obtained in some fashion. The two rode off on saddled horses that were waiting for them.

Newspapers at the time speculated that the county jailer had been bribed, saying it was a known fact that some citizens of Gallup had raised the necessary money. The reports did not identify the jailer by name, but there appears to be evidence that Elfego Baca was the jailer at the time.

The morning after the escape, a note was found on a jail windowsill, written by Charlie Ross and addressed to the editor of the *Albuquerque Daily Democrat*. The note read:

> *County Hotel, Jan. 3, 1887. To Mr. Roberts, of the Democrat: Please say in your paper that hearing there is a reward offered for my pardner Johnson, that I have gone to find him. Tell the boys not to feel uneasy about my absence, and as the weather is such that they might take cold, it may be better for their health to stay at home. We'll turn up in time, and doant [sic] you forget it. C. Henry Ross, with his hair parted in the middle.*

On the night of January 17, 1887, two weeks after his escape from jail, Ross led an abortive attempt to wreck and rob an eastbound Atlantic and Pacific passenger train about four miles west of Grants (or eighty miles west of Albuquerque). Trinkaus also was believed to have been involved. The *Democrat*, on January 19, told how the scheme was put into action:

A rail was unspiked from the track at a point where there is a heavy grade and where it would be impossible for an engineer to hold his engine. The rail was left in position to prevent attracting notice, and a stout lariat was attached to drag it from its place at the fatal moment. The passenger train which it was intended to victimize consisted of two Pullmans, the passenger coaches, an express and a baggage coach.

The passenger train was running from two to three hours late, however, and when a lone locomotive was seen approaching from the west at about nine o'clock, it was mistaken for the passenger train and wrecked, the engineer and fireman jumping out of the overturned cab and escaping on foot.

Railroad detectives learned a few days later that the bandits could be located at the Lail and Buoy ranch, about fifty miles west of Belen, and they rode to the ranch accompanied by posses from Albuquerque and Socorro. From places of concealment on the ranch, the possemen saw three armed men approaching on horseback and ordered them to throw up their hands. Two did, without hesitation, but the third reached for his gun and was shot down before he had a chance to use it. He died two hours later, after confessing his part in the attempted train robbery, and was buried on the ranch under a marker reading "Hardy Foster, train wrecker, Killed While Resisting Arrest, Jan. 27, 1887."

The two captives were taken before a Los Lunas justice of the peace, where they were identified as Charlie

Baca, who as district attorney had been campaigning to clean up drinking and gambling establishments and enforce the laws against prostitution and the carrying of firearms, answered that Mallet had been seen carrying a gun while singing in the church choir and at dances, where there were no Chinese present, and that he could find no territorial law that permitted a Chinese inspector to carry a deadly weapon.

Baca's critics contended that he caused the arrest of Mallet out of personal spite because the Chinese inspector, rather than Baca, had been invited to welcome the New Mexico governor at a livestock meeting in Socorro, to which Baca was not even invited. Although a Socorro jury convicted Mallet of the charge, the charge was eventually dismissed by a district judge.

Upon leaving the district attorney's office, Baca wrote, he was hired as a special prosecutor for a cattle association headquartered in Sierra County at a salary of $500 a month. He reportedly was successful in apprehending and prosecuting a number of cattle rustlers.

It was while he was serving as Socorro County clerk that Baca studied law in a private law office, as was a custom in those days, and was admitted to the bar.

William A. Keleher, Albuquerque attorney and historian, wrote in his *Memoirs, 1892–1969* published in 1969, that Baca was admitted to practice law in Socorro by District Judge A. A. Freeman after having read Smith's *Elementary Law* and a few chapters of Blackstone's *Commentaries*, which Keleher noted was "assuredly a scant preparation for the bar." Baca was admitted to the bar in December 1894, and two months later became a junior partner in the Socorro law firm of Freeman and Baca.

When interviewed in 1936 by Janet Smith of the WPA Writers' Program, Baca said that District Judge Charles A. Leland, when he was appointed to the bench in Socorro in 1898, hired him on a daily basis as an interpreter and bodyguard. He said that Judge Leland, from Toledo, Ohio, presided over a district that included Socorro, Lincoln, Chaves, and Eddy counties and had heard stories of continuing frontier violence in the region he served.

Baca said he accompanied the judge to Roswell, seat of Chaves County, and the two shared a large hotel room there. In a Roswell bar, he said, he met two Texans who owned a large sheep ranch, and they were complaining that they had posted a $2,000 bond for an elderly sheepherder from Mexico who had been engaged in a shooting scrape with another Mexican, that he was now due to appear in court, but that he had not been seen for three weeks.

"Two thousand bucks shot to hell," one of the ranchers said.

Baca said he asked them if it would be worth $500 to them for him to settle the case without forfeiting the bond, and they replied that it would. Baca asked for the money in advance, and they gave it to him in their hotel room that night.

Baca said he told Judge Leland about the case of the elderly Mexican without mentioning that he was missing and urged that the defendant be given a $50 fine rather than a jail sentence, saying that the Roswell schools were nearly broke and needed the money. The judge agreed to the fine.

Baca said he then walked around Roswell looking for an elderly Mexican who could not speak English, found

Elfego Baca (left) and some Roswell friends embarking on a sporting afternoon. (Courtesy of Museum of New Mexico, negative no. 87477).

one who was chopping wood, and asked him if he wanted a job. The Mexican replied that he had a job, chopping wood, and Baca told him that he could give him a job that would pay him $25 for a small amount of work. Baca told him that all he had to do was to appear in court with him, say the word *guilty* when a paper was read to him, and not say another word.

The Mexican agreed to the proposition.

At the appointed time, Baca and the woodchopper appeared in court before Judge Leland, the charge was read, and the Mexican said, "Guilty." The judge pronounced the $50 fine, and the Mexican said, "*Gracias.*"

The judge did not speak Spanish, but he knew that "*gracias*" meant "thank you," and it seemed to irritate him. According to Baca's story, this exchange then followed:

Judge: "I'm going to make you Mexicans obey the law in this country, and the next time I find you in my court I am going to send you to the penitentiary. Do you understand?"

Baca's translation: "The judge says that any time you Mexicans are not treated properly by the people of Roswell, you have only to let him know."

The Mexican: "*Gracias.*"

Judge: "Tell that Mexican that he has nothing to thank me for. Tell him I don't like his looks. He looks to me like an outlaw and an imposter. I should presume from his appearance that he has escaped from some other country where he has no doubt committed some crime. Tell him that he would do well to stay out of my court hereafter."

Baca's translation: "The judge says that he is very much impressed with your appearance. He also likes your courtroom manner. He sends his compliments to your mother."

The Mexican: "*Gracias.*"

The judge dismissed court, and Baca gave the Mexican $50 with which to pay the fine, and $25 for his work. As Baca was leaving the courtroom, the astonished sheep ranchers approached him, exclaiming, "That's not the man we put up the bond for!"

"What the hell do you care," Baca replied, "the case is settled, isn't it?"

Baca told friends that when he entered a Roswell restaurant and was told, "We don't serve Mexicans here," he drew a gun from his pocket and was quickly served the meal of his choice.

Even as a young attorney in Socorro, Baca continued to have some minor scrapes with the law. A court docket indicates that in 1896 he was charged in connection with "an election matter" during his run for mayor and with assaulting one William Martin.

In 1899, Baca released a statement to the *Socorro Chieftain* claiming that Estevan Baca, the Socorro postmaster, had attempted to persuade David Baca to kill him and that David Baca had given him a sworn statement to that effect. According to David Baca's statement, the news article said, the Socorro postmaster told him on May 9 that "this thief" (Elfego Baca) was trying to steal his land at San Antonio, about a dozen miles south of Socorro, and "I want you to do away with him." David said he refused, saying that it was "bad business."

David said the postmaster then told him, "I control the district attorney, and unless you put that fellow out of the way, your case will be the first on trial at the next term of court. I kept you out of the penitentiary the last term." Elfego said David gave the statement in his office on June 15, 1899, in the presence of Clemente Hightower and Ignacio A. Gutierres.

Several years later, Baca moved his law practice to El Paso, Texas, nearly two hundred miles south of Socorro, where he remained about two years. His business address in 1904 was listed as the Chambon Building, 211 1/2 San Antonio Street, El Paso. This was shortly before he was appointed district attorney in Socorro.

In 1907, following his employment as attorney and prosecutor for the cattle association, Baca moved his law practice to Albuquerque, establishing a residence at 401 North Sixth Street and offices in the N. T. Armijo Building, on the northwest corner of Railroad (now Central) Avenue and Second Street. The following year he formed a partnership with Lowell Loughary in the law firm of Baca and Loughary, which, among other things, dealt in gold, silver, and copper mining properties in New Mexico. Baca had long maintained an interest in mining and prospecting.

In 1911, on the eve of the admission of the Territory of New Mexico into the union as the forty-seventh state, the Republican Party nominated Baca and George Curry, a former governor of New Mexico, for election to the two seats New Mexico was entitled to in the United States House of Representatives. The nominating speech for Baca, delivered by Albert Bacon Fall of Otero County, was according to Curry "an eloquent tribute to the Spanish-Americans of New Mexico." Curry was elected, but Baca lost to Democrat Harvey B. Fergusson of Albuquerque.

Baca was credited with helping to ensure the selection of Fall as one of the new state's first United States senators during the first session of the Republican-controlled New Mexico State Legislature early in 1912. The legislature had been authorized to appoint the first two senators, and the top contenders were Fall, William H. "Bull" Andrews, and Thomas B. Catron, with only a few votes separating them.

Four Hispanic legislators who favored Andrews were lured by Baca to a Santa Fe hotel, where they were arrested for allegedly selling their votes. They were jailed for several days, during which time the remaining legislators, in close balloting, selected Fall and Catron as New Mexico's first senators.

The four jailed legislators were exonerated and released on evidence that Baca and several other prominent political figures had staged the arrests to keep them from voting for Andrews and thus ensuring Fall a narrow victory. Fall later served as secretary of the interior during the administration of President Warren G. Harding, during which time he was convicted of accepting a bribe in connection with the notorious Teapot Dome scandal.

In 1913, Baca was unsuccessful in seeking the Republican nomination again for election to the United States House of Representatives. It may have marked the beginning of his disillusionment with mainstream Republican politics.

It was in 1913 that William Keleher, then a newspaper reporter, first met Baca, writing in his *Memoirs* that Baca was serving as *bastonero*, or master of ceremonies, at the legal hanging in Albuquerque of Demecio Delgadillo, a native of Mexico, who had been convicted and sentenced to death on a charge of murdering an Albuquerque woman. Keleher wrote that Baca was "a veteran witness to hangings" and, in his role as *bastonero*, helped to make all the necessary arrangements, including the supervision of the erection and testing of the scaffold.

By this time Baca had established his law offices, living quarters, and a printing plant in a one-story building at 523 West Gold Avenue, on the northeast corner of Gold Avenue and South Sixth Street in Albuquerque. In the printing plant he published a weekly political newspaper, *La Opinion Publica* (Public Opinion), which he used to boost his political beliefs and aspirations. He also organized an independent political group called the Bolt and Nut Club and later published a small paper called *La Tuerca* (The Nut), jokingly listing subscription prices as $2 a year to good citizens, $5 a year to bootleggers, and $5 a month to Prohibition agents.

Baca also printed business cards that identified himself as both a lawyer and a private detective. One side of the card read "Elfego Baca, Attorney-At-Law, License to practice in all courts from Justice of the Peace in New Mexico to the United States Supreme Court. Fees moderate." The other side read "Elfego Baca, Private Detective, Discreet Shadowing Done, Civil and Criminal Investigations, Divorce Investigations Our Specialty."

Charged With Murder
and Conspiracy

I t did not take Elfego Baca long to become involved with various leaders of the Mexican Revolution that flared up south of the border in 1910 as a result of the long years of tyrannical rule by President Porfirio Diaz and that threw the country into a decade of military and guerrilla warfare, assassinations, and presidential coups.

According to the Crichton biography, Baca was in El Paso in 1911 when the Mexican revolutionary forces of Francisco I. Madero, commanded by Gen. Pascual Orozco, were converging on the Mexican city of Juarez, on the south bank of the Rio Grande opposite El Paso. Learning that Pancho Villa was a member of the attacking force, Baca was curious to know if he was the Mexican bandit he had met in Parral, Mexico, in 1906, while trailing a notorious American cattle thief south of the border. Baca said the bandit, using the name Pancho Jaime, had offered to sell him some stolen mules in Parral.

Baca said he crossed the river at El Paso, went to the rebel camp, met Pancho Villa there, and was convinced he was the Mexican bandit he had met five years before. Villa's true name, incidentally, was Doroteo Arango.

The Madero forces attacked Juarez on May 7, 1911, and in a three-day battle defeated the federal forces there and captured the city. As a result, the eighty-year-old President Diaz fled the country to France, and Madero assumed the presidency in Mexico City.

After the Juarez battle, Baca said, a messenger came to his room at the Zeigler Hotel in El Paso and told him that Col. Francisco "Pancho" Villa wanted to talk to him, and he was led at night to the entrance of an El Paso alley where Villa was waiting. Villa told Baca that he had certain valuables that he wanted to turn over to him for safekeeping and asked him to come to his headquarters in Juarez the next morning.

Baca said he was unable to keep the appointment the next day, as American troops had blocked all routes across the river into Mexico. Baca's failure to appear angered Villa, and his anger intensified when Baca "engineered a coup," as Baca vaguely put it, that resulted in Villa's losing one of his prized Mauser rifles, four of which had been hand-tooled for him at a cost of $1,000 each. Baca said Villa offered a $30,000 reward for him.

When Madero was ousted and executed in a counterrevolution in February 1913, the ruthless Gen. Victoriano Huerta seized power in Mexico. In a futile effort to gain recognition by the United States government, he hired Baca as his American representative, and Baca traveled to Washington, D.C., on at least one occasion on Huerta's behalf.

Meanwhile, an anti-Huerta movement was launched by Villa, Venustiana Carranza, and Alvaro Obregon. Among those loyal to Huerta was Gen. Jose Ynez Salazar, who had defeated Villa at Hidalgo del Parral in 1912. Salazar's troops were defeated by anti-Huerta forces near Juarez on November 25, 1913, and he retreated to Ojinaga, on the south bank of the Rio Grande southeast of Juarez, to assist in the defense of that city.

Ojinaga fell to Villa's troops on January 10, 1914,

In his later years, Elfego Baca proudly displays the rifle stolen from Pancho Villa. (Courtesy Museum of New Mexico, negative no. 87485).

causing a mass exodus of Huerta loyalists across the river into Texas, and Salazar was arrested on January 17 at Sanderson, Texas. He was taken to Fort Bliss at El Paso to face charges of violating United States neutrality laws designed to prevent Mexican revolutionists from seeking temporary refuge in the United States before returning to their revolutionary activities in Mexico.

Salazar also was charged with smuggling munitions of war across the border into Mexico. A federal jury in Santa Fe acquitted him of the smuggling charge on May 14, and he was taken to a detention camp at Fort Wingate, New Mexico, to face charges of violating the neutrality laws.

Salazar hired Baca to defend him and secure his release, and he instructed Baca to go to Washington, D.C., and meet with certain parties there concerning his fee. In Washington, Baca said later, he was escorted to a bank, where bank officials asked him to name his fee. Expecting to bargain, he suggested what he considered an exorbitant fee of $30,000, and was surprised when a cashier's check for that amount was handed to him. When told by a banker that he had been authorized to pay him any fee up to $100,000, Baca replied that he had been prepared to accept a much smaller fee than the amount given.

Baca prepared a writ of habeas corpus contending that Salazar was being held illegally by military authorities and that he was not held by any treaty nor charged with being a prisoner of war. After a court hearing on the matter, United States District Judge William H. Pope denied the petition for release and ordered Salazar back to Fort Wingate.

A federal grand jury then indicted Salazar for per-

Elfego Baca (left) with Gen. Jose Ynez Salazar (center) and Baca's secretary, J. B. McGinnis.

71

jury, alleging that he had not told the truth when he swore that he had not taken part in the battle at Ojinaga but had crossed the river into Texas prior to the battle to visit his wife and children in El Paso and had no intention of returning to Mexico. Salazar's trial on the perjury indictment was scheduled to be held in Albuquerque on November 30, 1914, and on November 16 he was taken to Albuquerque and placed in the two-story Bernalillo County Jail that stood on what is now the southwest corner of Central Avenue and Rio Grande Boulevard. His confinement proved to be a short one.

Four days later, at 9:30 on the evening of November 20, Albuquerque Police Judge George Craig and J. R. Galusha, a deputy United States marshal, were standing on a street corner in Albuquerque's downtown business section when Baca approached them on foot, took his watch from his pocket, and asked them what time they had. Both looked at their watches and said it was 9:30, and Baca asked them if they were sure their watches were correct, saying his showed a minute or two difference. Putting his watch back in his pocket, Baca walked away.

"Why do you suppose Elfego was haggling about exactly what time it is?" Galusha asked Craig.

The answer came a few minutes later when the bartender at the nearby White Elephant Saloon walked out of the saloon with a meat cleaver and began banging it against a metal lamp post, a loud and prearranged signal to policemen on their beats that there was an emergency and that they were to report to the police chief at once. The bartender had received a telephone call from the police station asking him to summon the officers, as Gen.

Jose Ynez Salazar had been "sprung" from the county jail at exactly 9:30.

Baca, Craig and Galusha now realized, had established an ironclad alibi by making them cognizant of the fact that he was not at the jail at 9:30 but had been talking to them on a street corner one and one-half miles to the east.

At the jail, Deputy Sheriff Carlos Armijo told authorities that he and Deputy Dolores Muniz were on duty there shortly before 9:30 when he received a telephone call that there had been a stabbing at the White Star Saloon on Indian School Road and that an officer was needed there. Armijo said he sent Muniz to the scene, then stretched out on a bed and began reading a book.

Moments later, Armijo continued, two men wearing knitted masks over their heads, with small openings for their eyes, appeared in the jail office after climbing over the board fence that surrounded the jail and entering through an unlocked back door.

"Give me Salazar, or you die," Armijo said one of the masked men warned him.

Armijo said he grabbed for his revolver, which was at the foot of his bed, when one of the men attacked him with a knife, slashing his hands and ripping his sweater open. He said he dropped his assailant with a right to the jaw, but was himself knocked down when the other man hit him on the back of his neck with a revolver.

The deputy said the two men handcuffed him to a post in the room, took some keys from a desk, and went upstairs to release Salazar. He said Salazar apparently anticipated their coming, as he had his suitcase packed and was ready to leave. The two released Salazar from his cell, and the three descended the stairs, went outside, and climbed over the

The Bernalillo County Jail as it existed in 1914 when Gen. Salazar escaped from it. (Courtesy of The Albuquerque Museum general collection, Phyliss Kirk donor).

fence, Armijo said, adding that he heard a car being cranked outside and that it backfired as it sped off to the east.

Armijo, still handcuffed to the post, yelled loud enough to attract the attention of M. L. Albers, who operated a store across the street from the jail. Albers entered the jail, found keys to unlock the handcuffs, and the two turned on the alarm, bringing officers to the scene. Deputy Muniz returned to the jail to report that there had been no stabbing at the White Star Saloon, leading to speculation that the telephone call was a hoax to rid the jail of one of its two deputies.

Armed posses, hastily organized, began searching Albuquerque and the surrounding countryside in automobiles, but no trace could be found of the Mexican general and his rescuers. A $100 reward offered by the federal government for information leading to the arrest of Salazar brought no response.

Months later, on April 10, 1915, a federal grand jury in Santa Fe returned an indictment charging Elfego Baca and five other individuals with conspiring against the United States to remove a federal prisoner from the custody of the United States marshal. Indicted, along with Baca, were Carlos Armijo, the deputy sheriff at the jail when Salazar was released; Manuel U. Vigil, the Bernalillo County district attorney; Trinidad C. de Baca, the state game warden; Monica Aranda; and Porfirio Saavedra. The indictment also identified Celestino Otero, who had died in the meantime, as a conspirator.

The indictment charged that Deputy Armijo had permitted Otero and Aranda to remove Salazar from the jail; that Salazar was driven off in a car by C. de Baca; that

Salazar was concealed in a tunnel beneath the patio at Vigil's ranch home at Alameda, just north of Albuquerque; and that he remained there until November 28, when Saavedra guided him on horseback south to the Mexican border, where the general crossed into Mexico.

More than two months before the conspiracy indictment was returned, on the afternoon of January 31, 1915, Elfego Baca shot alleged conspirator Celestino Otero to death on an El Paso street under mysterious circumstances. Baca surrendered to authorities, asked that he be indicted immediately, and issued a statement defending his actions that was published in El Paso and Albuquerque newspapers on February 2, 1915. The statement read:

> I came to El Paso several days ago in search of my son who disappeared from college at Las Cruces during the Christmas holidays, and thought it likely that I would be able to locate him here.
>
> Sunday afternoon, just as Dr. F. B. Romero and I were preparing to motor to the training camp of Jess Willard, Otero came into the lobby of the Paso del Norte where we were. I knew Otero but slightly in Albuquerque, but I greeted him and introduced him to Dr. Romero. Otero had his right hand in his overcoat pocket, and hesitated to shake hands. However, we treated him so cordially that he finally shook hands.
>
> Otero then asked if we could talk a little business with him. I told him that I could, and suggested that we go over into a corner of the lobby. This he declined to do, saying that he wanted to talk to me in private. I suggested that we go to my room, but he again objected. He thereupon proposed that I go to the saloon of M.

76

Andujo, intimating that Andujo desired to see me. I had secured the dismissal of the case of Andujo, who was indicted in New Mexico along with Jose Ynez Salazar, charged with the violation of the neutrality laws, after he had paid his bond and court costs in the federal court here, and a day or two ago had called upon him in regard to my fee as an attorney. I therefore presumed that Andujo desired to see me in connection with this matter and readily consented to the plan of Otero to go in the saloon.

We left the Paso del Norte and went around to the West San Antonio Street side where Dr. Romero's car stood. He [Otero] declined, saying he would walk to the place.

Dr. Romero and I then entered the automobile and drove in a roundabout way in order to give Otero time to reach Andujo's place of business. As we drove off Otero was joined by a Mexican, a young man who resembled Sylvestre Quevedo, a former officer of General Salazar's army, and for a time a prisoner at Fort Bliss, although I could not state positively that his companion was Quevedo.

Arriving in the vicinity of Andujo's place, we were detained for a moment by an engine crossing the street on the Santa Fe tracks. As we were about to move on we were hailed from the sidewalk by Otero and his companion. We turned the machine around and drew close to the sidewalk. As we did so Otero stepped forward and in Spanish made a vile remark about my mother. Saying this he drew back and drew a pistol from his pocket and fired. The bullet passed through my coat on the left side.

*Realizing that an attempt had been made on my
life, I pulled my pistol and shot twice. Otero fell back-
wards. After my second shot the man, lying on the
sidewalk, asked me not to shoot again, and I returned
my pistol to my pocket. Otero was ten feet from me at
the time.*

*Otero's companion hurried away from the scene
at the first shot. As I said, he resembled Sylvestre
Quevedo. While a prisoner he wrote me and asked if I
would take his case in the effort to secure his release.
At that time I was too busy on the Salazar case and
failed to reply to his letter.*

*I confidently believe that Otero intended to kill
me in the hotel. His hesitancy to shake hands and the
fact that he kept his hands in his overcoat led me to
believe that he was only deterred from shooting by the
cordiality with which he was received.*

Newspaper reports of the killing said that Otero's
automatic pistol jammed after he fired the first shot, which
tore through Baca's coat front near the second button, and
that Otero was attempting to shoot again when Baca fired
twice, both bullets striking Otero in the right side. Otero
died on the operating table at the police hospital about
fifteen minutes after he was shot.

"Custom House Inspector Biggs was the first American to reach the scene and saw Baca driving away," a news
report said. "Picking up Otero's pistol it discharged in his
hands. Eight cartridges remained when the weapon was
turned over to the police."

Baca and Dr. Romero drove to the El Paso home of
George Armijo in Palms Court on West Missouri Street,

where Baca called police and then surrendered himself, turning over the .32 Colt revolver with which he shot Otero. He was detained overnight and released the next morning on $7,500 bail. He retained El Paso attorney Harris Walthall to represent him. His request for an immediate indictment was granted within twenty-four hours.

"Baca was well known in El Paso where for two years he was a practicing attorney," the *El Paso Times* said.

The *Albuquerque Morning Journal*, in its report of the killing, made this comment:

> *In a country where, in the past, picturesque characters have been the rule rather than the exception, it is doubtful if a more picturesque character than Elfego Baca ever lived. A man of undoubted courage, he has lived through some of the most stirring events in the history of New Mexico, and there have been many occasions when his nerve was put to the supreme test.*

The article noted Baca's service as a Socorro County deputy sheriff, his fight with the cowboys at the Frisco Plaza, and his service with a Socorro County cattlemen's association, "in which capacity he is said practically to have broken up horse stealing in that county."

At a preliminary hearing in El Paso, an effort was made to show that Otero was unarmed when Baca shot him and that the gun found on the ground near his outstretched hand was placed there by Baca, who had obtained it from an El Paso pawnshop for that purpose. Later, an El Paso jury acquitted Baca of the murder charge, ruling that he shot in self-defense.

The Albuquerque newspaper said that Otero had been living at the Vigil ranch at Alameda as caretaker and described him as a well-educated Spaniard (indicating he was a native of Spain) who was in his forties and who sold patent medicine under the name Don Pedro Abeyta. The article said that he had been charged in Albuquerque with practicing medicine without a license and with attempting to kill Constable Monico Garcia of Martineztown by stabbing him with a pocketknife during an argument behind a saloon on North First Street. The newspaper said both charges had been dismissed.

The conspiracy trial of Baca and his codefendants opened before a federal jury in Santa Fe on December 15, 1915, United States District Judge John C. Pollock presiding. United States Attorney Summers Burkhart prosecuted the case, and the defense attorneys were A. B. Renehan and O. A. Larrazolo.

Burkhart said in his opening statement that the government would prove that Baca engineered the escape of Gen. Salazar and later murdered Celestino Otero. Defense attorneys objected to this statement, noting that Baca was not on trial for murder. It was agreed that in further references to Otero the prosecutor would use the word killed rather than the word murdered.

Burkhart said that Otero had talked freely about his part in the conspiracy and that Vigil had supplied money to send Otero out of the state following the escape. He said that C. de Baca had admitted to certain persons that he had taken part in the conspiracy.

The principal witness for the government was Otero's widow, Mrs. Ofelia Ortega de Otero, who testified that Baca was well acquainted with her late husband, had agreed to pay him $1,000 to take part in Salazar's escape, and had lured him to El Paso and murdered him when he demanded payment. She testified that Salazar had been hidden in a tunnel beneath the patio of Vigil's ranch home after his escape and that she saw C. de Baca visit Salazar there on two occasions.

Under cross-examination, Mrs. Otero said she had only her husband's word that Baca had agreed to give him $1,000 to help in the escape. The defense, in attempting to show that her general reputation was bad, asked her if she had been a prostitute both before and after her marriage.

"It's none of your business!" she exclaimed.

The defense introduced testimony that investigators could find no trace of a tunnel or other opening beneath the patio of Vigil's home. The government introduced into evidence a "cryptic" telegram that allegedly had been sent by Vigil to Dr. F. B. Romero at El Paso on January 29, 1915, shortly before the killing of Otero.

Deputy Armijo testified that the two masked men who entered the jail rolled their r's when speaking, in the custom of natives of Mexico. He denied government accusations that he had cut himself, or had asked somebody else to do it, to make it appear that he had been attacked by one of the intruders. Deputy Muniz told of being sent to the White Star Saloon on a false alarm.

Defense witnesses testified that they saw Baca and C. de Baca at the Graham Brothers Saloon in Albuquerque's downtown section from eight to ten o'clock on the evening of November 20 when Salazar was taken from the jail. Vigil testified that he was in Gallup, New Mexico, trying cases from November 16 to November 24.

Judge Pollock dismissed the conspiracy charges

against Saavedra and Armijo for lack of evidence, and the jury, composed entirely of Hispanic citizens of New Mexico, reported to the court on the evening of December 18 that they found the remaining defendants not guilty.

Later in his life, Baca answered criticism that he was "always acquitted by Spanish-American juries" by noting that the El Paso jury that acquitted him of murdering Otero did not include a single Spanish-American.

Crichton's 1928 biography of Baca claimed to tell for the first time the "true story" of Salazar's escape, a story entirely different from that alleged in the conspiracy indictment. Baca apparently was the source for this version, although he was not quoted directly, and there was no implication that he was involved in the escape.

According to the book, it was a group of prominent Mexican revolutionists, headed by Gen. Pascual Orozco, who rescued Salazar from the county jail. They reportedly were working for Huerta, who was seeking to regain the presidency of Mexico after having been ousted and forced into exile.

Gen. Orozco and eight other Mexican generals and a colonel disguised themselves as Mexican laborers and obtained roundtrip train tickets from El Paso to Colorado under the pretense that they were going to work in Colorado beet fields. After two days in Colorado, they boarded a southbound train and got off at Albuquerque at 7:30 on the evening of November 20, 1914, two hours before Salazar was released.

In Albuquerque they met two of Huerta's secret service agents, one of them an attractive young Mexican woman, who had arrived in the city earlier to lay the groundwork. The woman visited the county jail several times and drew a detailed map of the streets between the jail and the railroad depot.

Shortly before 9:30 that evening, the woman called the jail and asked that an officer be sent to a home on North Twelfth Street, saying a man was trying to break into the house. When one of the two deputies at the jail left to investigate the call, two of the Mexicans entered the jail, released Salazar, and drove him immediately east to the railroad depot, the street corners along the escape route guarded by the other Mexican revolutionists. All boarded a train that left for El Paso at 10:15 that night.

Baca's relationship with Salazar apparently ended with the Mexican general's escape from custody.

Salazar, upon his return to Mexico, led rebel forces that were defeated by Villa, then returned to New Mexico voluntarily to face the perjury charges against him. A federal jury acquitted him on December 9, 1915, and he returned to Mexico to join forces with his old enemy, Pancho Villa, in fighting against the forces of Gen. Venustiano Carranza, who had seized power upon the fall of Huerta in 1914.

In 1917, saying he was tired of fighting, Salazar left Villa and asked for amnesty. While riding horseback alone near a small Mexican village, he was shot dead by village guards, and his body was reportedly dumped down an abandoned well.

The Socorro County Courthouse and Jail (at rear) as they existed when Elfego Baca was the Socorro County sheriff. (Courtesy Museum of New Mexico, negative no. 14804).

Sheriff and Chief Bouncer

William Keleher, the lawyer and historian, was driving Elfego Baca through the western part of Socorro County in the 1930s when Baca said to him, "See the point of that hill over there? Well, I shot a man there once."

Keleher stopped the car, pulled a pencil and notebook from his pocket, and asked, "What was his name?"

"Hell, I was shootin', not taking a census," Baca replied gruffly.

Other details lacking, the incident Baca referred to may have occurred while he was serving a two-year term as sheriff of Socorro County in 1919 and 1920. As sheriff, his reputation was such that he did not have to travel around the county arresting persons charged with offenses but got them to come in merely by sending them letters that he said read something like this:

Dear Sir: I have a warrant here for your arrest. Please come in by March 15 and give yourself up. If you don't, I'll know that you intend to resist arrest, and I will feel justified in shooting you on sight when I come after you. Yours truly, Elfego Baca, sheriff.

Baca said that not one person receiving such a letter failed to appear at the appointed time.

Baca said that only one prisoner, a cattle thief from Texas, escaped from the county jail while he was sheriff but that his freedom did not last long. He said he released another prisoner, also from Texas, gave him a badge, a gun, and handcuffs, and told him to go find the escaped prisoner, his former cellmate, and bring him back. He said the released prisoner captured the escapee near the Arizona border, more than one hundred and fifty miles to the west, and brought him back.

Baca said he also took it upon himself to release eleven sheepherders who had been jailed merely because they owed small amounts of money to their employers that they could not pay. He said this cut down the jail's food bill.

Robert W. "Bob" Lewis, a pioneer New Mexico rancher and lawman, recalled in a 1949 interview that he once got into a little trouble at Socorro and was thrown in jail.

"I'll never forget how mad I was at Elfego Baca, the sheriff," he said. "He came around to my cell and insisted that I pay him rent for my lodgings."

In his political pamphlet, Baca told how he saved the county some money in the building of a county garage:

> In the two years previous to the day he was made sheriff of the county, the county was paying $100.00 a month for a garage. Mr. Baca saw that he could build a garage estimated to the value of $8000.00, and to build the same he decided on the following plan: To arrest all tramps and put them to work on the garage. Among those he caught were stonemasons, adobemakers, adobe-layers, plasterers, carpenters and painters.

As sheriff, Baca was criticized by some for being too friendly and lenient with Henry Coleman, a notorious rancher and gunman in the western part of the county who had been indicted on a murder charge. Coleman, whose real name was Henry Street Hudspeth, had long been considered the "black sheep" of a prominent Texas family.

Coleman was charged with the fatal shooting of Frank Bourbonnaise, who was among the suspects in the double murder of Coleman's estranged wife, Clara Coleman, and her hired hand, Don Oliver, both found shot to death in her ranch home south of the village of Quemado on December 12, 1918. Bourbonnaise was said to have been a convicted murderer who was on parole from Oklahoma when he was killed.

Former Gov. George Curry wrote in his autobiography that he was operating the Park Hotel in Socorro when Sheriff Baca brought Coleman to the hotel and insisted that he be given a room there, even though the court had ordered that he be held in jail without bail. Curry said Baca gave as his excuse that he did not believe Coleman was guilty of the murder charge.

Curry wrote that he gave Coleman a room in the hotel after taking his gun, which Baca had permitted him to carry, and locking it in a drawer in his office. The day before his trial, Curry continued, Coleman embarked on a drinking spree, got his gun from the drawer that Curry carelessly had left unlocked, and, waving the gun, said he was on his way to kill Harry Owen, the district attorney. Curry said he took the gun away from Coleman, locked him in his room, and sent for Baca, demanding that Coleman be put in jail where he belonged.

"He [Baca] let his friendship for Coleman lead him into a clear evasion of his official duty," Curry wrote, adding that Baca became his personal and political enemy for a while. Curry, who had served as sheriff of Lincoln County in the early 1890s, also wrote that "Elfego Baca was never a man to underrate in a physical encounter" and "there never was any question of Baca's personal courage."

Coleman, who was tried and acquitted of the murder charge, was shot to death in October 1921 by a five-man posse that went to his ranch at Goat Springs, northwest of Quemado, to serve a warrant charging him with stealing cattle. This was after Baca left office. An autopsy indicated that the fatal bullet was fired by rancher John "Salty John" Cox, Coleman's deadliest enemy, even though the two had been friends twenty-five years before when Cox attempted to rescue Coleman from the Juarez jail by throwing a rope over the high wall, only to find that his rented livery stable horse, unlike a roping horse, would not pull Coleman over the wall.

Asked in 1954 about the killing of Coleman, Cox, then an Albuquerque resident, would only say, "Some of us went out to his ranch one day and brought him out feet foremost." Although Cox and others believed that Coleman arranged the murders of his wife and her hired hand, the double murder remains an unsolved mystery.

Baca, defeated in his bid for reelection as Socorro County sheriff, soon returned to his law practice in Albuquerque.

Before returning to Albuquerque, however, Baca was employed briefly by the Tivoli, a large gambling hall in Juarez, Mexico, as "chief bouncer" in charge of a fourteen-member gambling hall police force. He told Crichton he received a salary of $750 a month, plus room and board and an automobile with chauffeur. When opera star Mary Garden visited the gambling hall, he escorted her around the Mexican city.

Prior to his employment at the Tivoli, Baca said, the leader of the Juarez underworld, a gang leader known as *Numero Ocho* (Number Eight), periodically raided the gambling hall with his followers and made off with large sums of cash. To prevent further such occurrences, Baca said, he traced *Numero Ocho* to his lair in a Juarez cellar; slapped, punched, and kicked him around; and warned him and members of his gang at gunpoint to stay away from the Tivoli. They did, and the gambling hall had no more trouble with them while Baca was there.

Baca said his employment at the Tivoli came to an abrupt end when he made the mistake of jailing the son of the Juarez chief of police.

Baca was then employed briefly by the United States Department of the Interior as an Indian and land agent, thanks to his old political friend, Albert Bacon Fall, recently appointed secretary of the interior by President Warren G. Harding. In this role Baca was sent to southeastern Utah, where he helped to mediate a serious dispute between Paiute Indians and some white ranchers.

Elfego Baca as a sixty-two-year-old lawyer in Albuquerque, New Mexico. (Courtesy Museum of New Mexico, negative no. 87489).

The Perennial Candidate

Elfego Baca moved back to Albuquerque from Socorro in 1922, establishing a residence at 315 West Marquette Avenue and law offices in the Stern Building at the southwest corner of Central Avenue and Fourth Street. In 1924 he moved his offices to rooms 304 and 306 in the new, six-story Sunshine Building, which had just been completed at the southeast corner of Central Avenue and Second Street.

Although Baca's single term as sheriff of Socorro County was the last elective office he held, he spent the remaining twenty-five years of his life seeking election to other public offices. A loyal Republican for most of his life, he claimed from time to time that the Republicans "double-crossed" him, and he formed independent, progressive Republican clubs. It was reported that both Republican and Democratic leaders, when finding it advantageous to have an Hispanic candidate on their tickets, persuaded Baca to seek certain offices by offering him financial support, often regarding him as more of a "spoiler" than a serious candidate.

Such was the case in 1924 when the Democratic Party persuaded Baca to seek the Democratic nomination for election as judge of the Second Judicial District, comprising Bernalillo and Sandoval counties. It was then that Baca issued the first version of his popular political pamphlet, outlining his platform and giving a sketch of his life.

"If elected, I will use my judicial capacity without taking into consideration politics, nationality or religion of the litigants involved," he wrote.

He said he opposed suspended sentences upon entry of guilty pleas, asserted he would recognize no bosses, pledged that no "third-degree" methods would be allowed, and promised to provide attorneys with an office in the courthouse where they could converse with their clients.

"If I am elected, the district attorney will not be permitted to talk to people in jail charged with committing a crime," he wrote, adding that he would not permit a sheriff to have deputies listen to a conversation between a defendant and his attorney.

Baca, although sometimes running a close race, was unsuccessful in this and all future attempts to win public office.

In 1925, Baca established his office and living quarters once again in the one-story building he owned at Sixth Street and Gold Avenue. Now sixty years old, his fortunes began a steady decline. He was forced into bankruptcy, sought outside jobs to supplement his income, and began drinking heavily. In 1930, he opened a small restaurant in his building, the Elfego Cafe, which lasted only a short time.

Baca complained to friends that the closeness of his office and living quarters posed a domestic problem, explaining that his wife, Francisquita, often entered his private office unannounced while he was conferring with clients. He considered getting a restraining order prohibiting her from doing so but was talked out of it by his friend and informal adviser William Keleher.

Baca and his wife soon became separated, she moving to San Diego, California, where she was living in 1932, apparently with one of their six grown children. She later returned to his household.

United States District Judge Colin Neblett, who like many judges was willing to overlook Baca's informal and often unorthodox courtroom manners and procedures, often appointed him to defend persons charged with bootlegging or with illegally selling liquor to Indians. The story is told that on one such occasion, while Baca was defending a man charged with selling whisky to an Indian, he held up the unopened and sealed whisky bottle that the government had introduced into evidence, turned to the jury, and asked: "Do you see this bottle? The label says it contains whisky. But how can we be sure? Did anybody taste it? No. Did anybody smell it? No. If I put a sign on my back saying I am Jesus Christ, does that make me the Saviour?"

The federal judge held back a smile and let the case go to the jury.

Baca (as well as the judge) was not averse to drinking bootleg whisky during the Prohibition era, however, and he hosted small gatherings at his living quarters on Sunday afternoons during which he and his friends played poker and drank bootleg whisky.

Lauro E. Flores, who was a member of this inner circle, recalled that he felt uncomfortable playing poker with Baca, as he always kept his gun on the table. He said Baca was never without his gun, even wearing it fastened to a gun belt in the Old West style while relaxing at his favorite Albuquerque pool hall.

"He explained that he had enemies, and that it was illegal to carry a concealed weapon," Flores said.

Baca's reputation as a frontier gunfighter stayed with him all his life, and he often put it to good advantage. When a bill collector or another unwelcome guest confronted him in his law office, he would open a desk drawer, pull a six-shooter from it and place it on the desk, and continue shuffling papers in the drawer. When he looked up again, the unwelcome visitor usually had disappeared.

When a fire damaged his Albuquerque printing plant, Baca put in an insurance claim for $1,200. An insurance adjuster from Denver arrived in Albuquerque and told Baca he would give him only $600, "take it or leave it." Baca sent word to the Denver visitor, through his friend William Keleher, that if he did not have the $1,200 by noon that day, he would find himself dead in the middle of Central Avenue. Word came shortly before noon that the $1,200 had been deposited for Baca at his bank.

When the Albuquerque bank Baca patronized failed and closed its doors, Baca entered the bank and at gunpoint forced a bank official to hand over the $500 he had on deposit there. When an Albuquerque grocer heard of Baca's success in withdrawing his money, he tried the same thing and wound up in jail.

While walking along an Albuquerque street one day, Baca drew his gun and shot a dog that darted out of a yard and attacked him. When the dog's owner came out and began berating Baca, he threatened to shoot him, too.

Although Baca had a giant reputation at the time, he was anything but a giant in appearance, and those meeting him for the first time were often surprised to find that he was a short man, wearing eyeglasses, with a big belly and a mischievous twinkle in his eyes.

On January 1, 1934, Baca announced that he was a candidate for the Republican nomination for governor of

New Mexico. In doing so, he issued what he called his "Manifesto," a small pamphlet outlining what he intended to do if elected.

Baca said in his manifesto that he would "pass a law for the purpose of reducing the taxes of taxpayers to one-half of what the taxpayers are paying now" and that he would reduce the license fees for automobiles, trucks, and other vehicles to five dollars a year.

"I am in favor of repealing the method of collecting taxes by the County Treasurers, that is by sending each taxpayer a notice that he is delinquent," Baca said. "It is a big expense to the counties, and each individual knows without receiving notice that he has not paid his taxes."

He said he would prohibit district attorneys and their assistants from handling civil cases, saying this was not fair to the rest of the lawyers in the state, as 90 percent of civil cases were handled by the district attorney offices.

"I am in favor of a law requiring the Sheriff to have not more than one deputy in each precinct for this reason, in some precincts of the counties there are more deputies than it is necessary, and I have noticed that the deputies are the ones that cause the disturbances in dances, etc., on account of their badges," he said.

Baca said he would have the sheriffs check all automobiles and trucks in New Mexico having out-of-state licenses, as there were "too many outlaws coming into and going through New Mexico without being molested by any peace officer." He said he would repeal the law that prohibited the carrying of deadly weapons, saying that, "outlaws carry a gun anyhow and the good citizens cannot carry one to protect themselves."

If elected, he continued, he would pardon a prisoner

from the state penitentiary each Saturday, saying that there were more than six hundred prisoners in the penitentiary "at big expense to the state" and that 75 percent of them were convicted because they did not have adequate legal counsel. He said he would create a lawyer to defend poor people charged with criminal offenses and would repeal capital punishment.

Baca said he would propose license fees for any person running a game, adding that "now there is no law requiring gamblers to pay a license, but they are gambling just the same."

Baca said he supported the establishment of a state fair in Albuquerque each year, that he would revive the mounted police force in New Mexico, and that he would prohibit county clerks from issuing marriage licenses to any couple who did not produce a doctor's certificate of health.

In the elections that fall, Clyde Tingley, a Democrat, was elected governor of New Mexico.

Baca had allied himself politically with United States Senator Bronson M. Cutting of New Mexico, a progressive, liberal Republican who spoke fluent Spanish and who was regarded as a champion of the Hispanic citizens of New Mexico. A member of a wealthy family of Long Island, New York, he settled in Santa Fe in 1910, following his graduation from Harvard, and purchased the *New Mexican*, Santa Fe's daily newspaper. Cutting was appointed to the United States Senate in 1927 by Gov. Richard C. Dillon and won election to the seat in 1928. His senatorial career came to an end on May 6, 1935, when he was killed in an airplane crash in Missouri.

Baca's high regard for Cutting is reflected in a letter he wrote to Tom McGrath of Roy, New Mexico, on

February 9, 1934. The letter read:

> My dear Sir: In the Albuquerque Morning Jour-
> nal, this morning, I read your article which is in
> reference to the meeting held by the so called Old Guard
> Republicans, and in do [sic] justice to you and to the
> public at large, I can't help to extend to you my con-
> gratulations for such article. In this connection I desire
> to say to you that I wish New Mexico had at least
> twenty men of the caliber and who has the interest of
> the people of New Mexico at heart as Senator Bronson
> M. Cutting has had, politically and otherwise.
>
> No person who is so well acquaintanced with
> Senator Cutting, as I am, can't [sic] denied that Sena-
> tor B.M. Cutting is what I should called [sic] a presi-
> dential timber.
>
> With kindly regards believe me to be, Very truly
> yours, Elfego Baca.

In November 1935, six months after Cutting's death,
the Cutting estate filed suit in Bernalillo County District
Court seeking to eject Baca from his residential and office
building at Sixth and Gold, contending that Cutting had
purchased the property for $7,000 in 1924, when Baca was
adjudged bankrupt, and had held title to it since that time.
Baca answered that Cutting, who was well known for
being quite generous to his friends and supporters, had
taken possession of the property to save him (Baca) from
financial ruin and had held the title as trustee for Baca with
the promise that Baca could redeem the property at any
time upon repayment of the money Cutting had advanced
for the deed of conveyance, plus interest, taxes, insurance

premiums, and maintenance costs.

Baca, represented by the Keleher law firm, also alleged that the Cutting estate owed him $44,000 for detective work he said he had performed for Cutting, during which time, he claimed, he had furnished Cutting detailed information on political affairs in New Mexico. The complicated litigation was settled out of court, and Baca was given the deed to the disputed property. Although Cutting, in his will, forgave his many debtors, listing them by name, he had either ignored or overlooked Baca's debt on the property.

Robert J. Nordhaus, an attorney with the Keleher firm, said he sometimes had difficulty communicating with Baca during the course of the litigation, that being ushered into Baca's living quarters he would find him lying on his bed, moaning and groaning, with a bottle of whisky in one hand and a gun in the other. A nineteenth-century New Mexican struggling to survive in the twentieth century.

In 1940, Baca was again unsuccessful in seeking election as district judge. In this race he issued a slightly revised version of his 1924 political and biographical pamphlet, in both English and Spanish language versions, which he sold for ten cents a copy.

Baca observed his seventy-fifth birthday in 1940 by making a pilgrimage to Socorro, his hometown, where he was presented the key and the door to the jail cell in which he had been held prisoner in 1884 following his gun battles with the cowboys at the Frisco Plazas, the old jail having recently been demolished. Baca claimed that he was the first prisoner in the jail, which had still been under construction when he was lodged there in 1884.

The *Albuquerque Tribune,* in a birthday tribute to
Baca, said that his stormy career resembled a Western
novel and that he "possibly has dodged more lead in the
form of six-shooter and rifle bullets than any person in
New Mexico." The article added that Baca "has lived
through many hair-raising experiences [and] can't recall
the number of times he has stared death in the face and
emerged alive with both six-shooters smoking."

Baca told the newspaper that he always was at his
best as a prosecutor but boasted that he had defended
thirty persons charged with murder and only one went to
the penitentiary, and that was only because another attorney was associated with him in the defense.

There may have been other reasons, too. Montague
Stevens, the pioneer Socorro County rancher, said in 1953
that he had an Hispanic sheepherder working for him in
the early days who always had a bit more money than he
paid him but who would not tell where the extra money
was coming from. Finally, after much persuasion, he
agreed to tell Stevens about the extra income, on the
condition that Stevens not tell anybody.

"Do you know Elfego Baca, the lawyer in Socorro?"
the sheepherder asked. "Well, I am on the jury there, and
Elfego sends me some money every month, and each time
he has a case in court, I am always on his side."

Having at least one juror in your pocket was not an un-
common practice among New Mexico lawyers at the time.

In 1943, Baca opened yet another business enterprise
at his office and residence, which he called Elfego Baca's Im-
ported Goods Store. When two men representing the federal government entered his office to discuss condemning
his property for the erection of a federal office building,

Late in his life, Elfego Baca poses with a gun in each hand. (Courtesy Museum of New Mexico, negative no. 128796).

Baca picked up two six-shooters and ordered them to leave. They left in a hurry.

In 1944, at the age of seventy-nine and in failing health, Baca moved from the corner he had occupied off and on for thirty years and established his residence and office at 1501 North Third Street. He announced that he was a Democratic candidate for district attorney and issued a pamphlet entitled *Political Record of Elfego Baca and a brief history of his life,* which he sold for fifty cents a copy.

"My investigator for the District Attorney's office shall work under my instructions and no others," he wrote in the pamphlet. "He would not be permitted to become a self-made newspaper reporter. The district attorney investigator is equivalent to a detective, and [should] not say in the newspapers what he is going to do and accomplish nothing."

Baca was again unsuccessful in this, his last try, for election to public office. Now in the twilight of his life, he kept expressing one major ambition: that his eventful life be made the subject of a motion picture. No one seemed interested.

About ten o'clock on the evening of August 27, 1945, Baca died peacefully at his home at the age of eighty. Mrs. Baca wrote to former United States Representative Clinton P. Anderson of New Mexico, who several weeks before had been appointed secretary of agriculture by President Harry Truman, that her husband had always had the highest respect for him and died while waiting to hear him speak on the radio.

Albuquerque newspapers, calling Baca one of New Mexico's last links with the frontier era, identified his survivors as his wife; a son, George Baca of Wapato,

Washington; five daughters, Miss Frances Baca of Albuquerque, Mrs. Lucille Levey of San Francisco, California, Mrs. Jean Bernard of Cajon, California, Mrs. D. N. Talbott, and Mrs. Sofia Cardena of San Diego, California; eight grandchildren; and two great-grandchildren.

Funeral services were held August 31 at Albuquerque's Immaculate Conception Catholic Church, with the Rev. Patrick J. Keleher officiating. Pallbearers were listed as William A. Keleher, Ernest Polansky, Harold Waggoner, M. J. McGuinness, and Joseph L. Smith, all Albuquerque lawyers, and John A. Flaska, Bernalillo County assessor and soon to become sheriff. Burial services were held in Albuquerque's Sunset Memorial Park.

The *Albuquerque Journal*, in telling of Baca's death, quoted him as having said that he had killed nine men and wounded eight others during his life, listing those killed as four cowboys at the Frisco Plazas, Celestino Otero at El Paso, and four other unidentified persons, who, he had explained with a chuckle, were "unofficial."

In the 1950s, Baca's longtime residential and office building at Sixth and Gold was demolished to make way for construction of an eight-story federal office building. During the excavation work, a revolver was found under the floor of Baca's former building.

In 1959, a Walt Disney film crew arrived in New Mexico to begin filming a television series, "The Nine Lives of Elfego Baca," which was telecast to nationwide audiences. Baca would have loved that, even though he might not have recognized himself as portrayed. He was at peace in the Albuquerque cemetery, where he lies today, beneath a simple headstone reading, "Elfego Baca. 1865–1945."

SOURCES

Books

Albuquerque City Directories, 1907–1945.

Ball, Larry D. *Elfego Baca in Life and Legend*. El Paso: Texas Western Press, 1992.

Beckett, V. B. *Baca's Battle*. Houston: Stagecoach Press, 1962.

Cook, James H. *Fifty Years on the Old Frontier*. Norman: University of Oklahoma Press, 1957.

Crichton, Kyle S. *Law and Order Ltd.: The Rousing Life of Elfego Baca*. Santa Fe: The New Mexican Publishing Corporation, 1928.

Curry, George. *George Curry, 1861–1947: An Autobiography*. Edited by H. B. Hening. Albuquerque: University of New Mexico Press, 1958.

French, William. *Some Recollections of a Western Ranchman*. New York: Argosy-Antiquarian Ltd., 1965.

An Illustrated History of New Mexico. Chicago: Lewis Publishing Company, 1895.

Keleher, William A. *Memoirs: 1892–1969*. Santa Fe: Rydal Press, 1969.

Larson, Robert W. *New Mexico's Quest for Statehood, 1846–1912*. Albuquerque: University of New Mexico Press, 1968.

Who's Who in New Mexico. Albuquerque: The Abousleman Company, 1937.

Articles

Fitzpatrick, George. "The Real Elfego Baca." *New Mexico Magazine* April, May 1960.

Jewell, Mel. "Outlaw Born Too Late." (Henry Coleman). *New Mex-*